P9-DFQ-860

Smart Office
Organizing

Smart Office Organizing

Simple Strategies for Bringing
Order to Your Workspace

Sandra Felton
and Marsha Sims

Revell
a division of Baker Publishing Group
Grand Rapids, Michigan

© 2011 by Sandra Felton and Marsha Sims

Published by Revell
a division of Baker Publishing Group
P.O. Box 6287, Grand Rapids, MI 49516-6287
www.revellbooks.com

Printed in the United States of America

All rights reserved. No part of this publication may be reproduced, stored in a retrieval system, or transmitted in any form or by any means—for example, electronic, photocopy, recording—without the prior written permission of the publisher. The only exception is brief quotations in printed reviews.

Library of Congress Cataloging-in-Publication Data
Felton, Sandra.
     Smart office organizing : simple strategies for bringing order to your work-space / Sandra Felton and Marsha Sims.
        p.   cm.
     Includes bibliographical references.
     ISBN 978-0-8007-2010-0 (pbk.)
     1. Work environment. 2. Orderliness. 3. Organization. I. Sims, Marsha.
     II. Title.
     HD7261.F45 2011
     650.1—dc23   2011014072

Unless otherwise indicated, Scripture is taken from the New American Standard Bible®, copyright © 1960, 1962, 1963, 1968, 1971, 1972, 1973, 1975, 1977, 1995 by The Lockman Foundation. Used by permission.

To protect the privacy of those who have shared their stories with the authors, some details and names have been changed.

Any internet addresses, email addresses, and phone numbers in this book are accurate at the time of publication. They are provided only as a resource; Baker Publishing Group does not endorse them or vouch for their content or permanence.

11   12   13   14   15   16   17   7   6   5   4   3   2   1

In keeping with biblical principles of creation stewardship, Baker Publishing Group advocates the responsible use of our natural resources. As a member of the Green Press Initiative, our company uses recycled paper when possible. The text paper of this book is composed in part of post-consumer waste.

This book is dedicated to all of the wonderful disorganized people who have allowed us, hopefully and fearfully, into the hallowed ground of their offices and homes. Over the last twenty-plus years, they have allowed us to touch their things, especially their papers, and have trusted us to make their confusion better.

This book is further dedicated to those people who, by reading our other books on the topic of organizing, have allowed us into the hallowed ground of their thinking. We have respectfully challenged the thoughts and feelings that have led them into chaos with their papers and belongings. Hopefully they have come out the other side of that challenge better able to face the fearsome task of making positive changes to very basic parts of their lives.

In short, this book is dedicated to the amazing people who, like us, struggle to bring order and sanity into their lives, especially in the area of that powerhouse place of life's business—the office.

Contents

Acknowledgments

"Whoop-de-do!" and "Yahoo!" to Nanette Holt, editor extraordinaire, who dared to dive into the depths of our writing and drag us, gasping and struggling, safely to the shores of writing sanity. This is our dramatic way of saying, "Thanks, Nanette, for all you did to set us in the right direction and keep us going there!"

A special thanks to all the good, hardworking folks at Revell, especially Lonnie Hull DuPont, for the confidence you place in us each time you say yes to a proposal for a new book on organizing. Together we have covered many aspects of this dynamic subject, and helped many of those who seek to bring order into their lives. It has been a great team effort.

Introduction

This book is not written for the executive who sits in a pristine space with a glass top desk and an assistant hovering about to keep the ragged ends of commerce neatly tucked. Nor is it for those who work in their own nicely controlled home offices, efficiently turning out projects with a minimum of effort. It is not even for the secretary at her desk behind the scenes, doing the same activity over and over and successfully producing a large body of work because her path is well-worn and carefully followed. All of these workers have a system already set up and have found a way to work it.

This book is written for the rest of us, those whose lives are made up of a wide variety of activities that we happily pursue in that space we've dedicated to our work and call . . . our office. For the most part, our personalities are outgoing, spontaneous, and upbeat. We are not known for our efficiency. But despite our easy-going approach to life, we're surprisingly capable in completing assignments and following through on projects.

To keep up with our many activities and do them well, we increasingly need to come to grips with what is happening in our workspace. Managing the details of office work is not our strong suit. In order to compensate for this natural lack, we buy books on office organizing and hope that more instruction will lift the burden of confusion that tends to creep in as we work. We hope these books will free us to work with less effort in our own flexible style.

But sometimes we need more than another how-to. Sometimes we need to know why—why we struggle to hold things together in an organized way, when others seem to accomplish it with ease, quite naturally and with great success.

So before we give you our "how-tos" that will help you conquer disorganization for good, we're going to give you the "whys"—so the positive changes you make will last.

Why Office Organizing Books Don't Work . . . and the Paper Challenge

The office's basic job is to handle information coming by phone, fax, email, computer, and . . . paper. Ah, yes. Paper.

Paper is where the jam-up comes. Getting it, using it, and if necessary, storing it. The office is basically the throne room of King Paper. And at some point in the process, while we think paper is serving *us*, if we are not careful we end up serving *it*!

The question is: How can we be restored to our rightful position as rulers of our space, time, activities, and paper management? That's what this book is all about.

Books on office organizing tend to be dry and dusty— about as fun to read as the owner's manual for your copier. Nonetheless, people suffer through reading them.

We used to do it too. Like you, we were desperate for help in setting up our offices to handle the wonderful work we envisioned we would produce there. We gratefully read, looking for help from those who knew enough to give guidance and cared enough to share it.

And we suffered through—eventually learning how to make our offices work for us, and mastering those skills well enough to share them with others. Many thousands of others.

Through that, we also learned that books on office organizing don't have to be dull. They can be vibrant—and should be—because organizing your office is an exciting part of your plan to upgrade and organize your life and business.

Research shows that people learn by observing the actions of others. In our approach, you will be stimulated by true stories of real people. Each story takes you into a world very much like your own. As you engage with their experiences, you'll begin to see how you can move your office into the condition you want—but didn't believe you could achieve.

All of us tend to mirror what we observe, whether it's actually seen or just imagined as we read. As you read this book, you'll see Brad gaining control of his office by drawing an organizing schematic in chapter 5. You'll cheer for Erin as she develops an office that looks as professional as she is in chapter 7. In chapter 13, you'll see the secrets to Phyllis's and Juan's success in creating space for a nicely set up mini office at home. And you'll admire Eileen's perseverance in chapters 6 and 10 as she tackles the overwhelming clutter in her home office and finally develops a filing system that really works.

As you experience their solutions, pathways of order in your own mind will begin to develop. Rightly applied, those paths can lead you to the kind of environment where you want to work. In short, you will have power to create the office you want and need—and maintain it. An office that looks good and really "works"—can it get better than that?

Sprinkled with fun and full of solutions, this book leads you into the lives of others who have walked the path before you and come out the better for it. We (Marsha and Sandra) are your experienced guides, and we'll spotlight the important points along the way that will change your office life forever. Each chapter begins with Action Highlights to clue you in as to what it will cover, and ends with Smart Steps in the Right Direction to get you moving.

Whether your office is in your home or at an office building, yours alone or part of a large corporation, if you want good, solid solutions to your problems, this book is for you. We welcome you aboard and look forward to sharing this journey with you.

Now, let's get down to business with your first mini-quiz. You'll find one before each chapter. They'll help you assess the areas where you need the most help getting organized. So here goes. . . .

Mini-Quiz

1. Are you a people person?

2. Have you wondered why organizing is hard for you?

3. Would you like some quick solutions that will help?

If you answered "yes" to any of the above, grab a pencil, get comfy, and enjoy the eye-openers in chapter 1. They'll help you understand just why you've been fighting a never-ending battle with disorganization—and show what you can do to get a handle on it fast!

1

Why We Do What We Do

Change from the Inside Out

God give us the grace to accept with serenity the things that cannot be changed; courage to change the things that should be changed; and the wisdom to distinguish the one from the other.

Reinhold Niebuhr

Not everything that is faced can be changed, but nothing can be changed until it is faced.

James Baldwin

Action Highlights

By the end of this chapter, you'll be able to:

- Identify factors that make organizing difficult for you.
- Act on "quick fixes" that will jumpstart your organization project.

Disorganized people are often warm, sensitive, caring, and empathetic. If you're the disorganized type, you're probably casual, fun-loving, creative—and cluttered.

Don't beat yourself up about it. Be of good cheer! By committing to a few significant changes, you can become more organized. Really!

Now, the characteristics that make you prone to disorganization might not change. But we'll teach you how to adjust to them so they won't hold you back the way they do now. You can learn more about this in Sandra's book *Organizing for Life: Declutter Your Mind to Declutter Your World.*

Most significant causes of disorganization—in the office or elsewhere in life—are rooted deeply within us. That's why some people are able to maintain order during even the most difficult circumstances and others can't seem to hold their act together at any time, even when circumstances are optimal. Naturally neat folks are not likely to be reading this book, and may wonder why anybody would pick it up. Organizing is easy for them. But what about for you?

Let's peek into the lives of a few people for whom organizing does not come so easy. Maybe their stories will sound familiar. If you're open to acknowledging the similarities, and you're willing to take action, you'll see big changes. Let's get going.

How Your Personality Helps Create Clutter, and What You Can Do about It

Clutter grows in several types of soil. Identifying the characteristics within you that allow clutter to take root will help you weed them out.

Before we tackle the long-term solutions outlined in this book, you can begin to enjoy the relief that immediate improvements can bring. Just try quick fixes for these common clutter-causing characteristics:

- **Oblivious to the need for storage areas.** Obviously, if there's no place to put stuff, it will pile up and look messy. Interestingly, the chronic clutterer is often oblivious to the fact that lack of storage can be a major source of messiness problems. Consider Claire, who's notoriously neat, and always stops to think about whether she has room for something *before* she buys it. In contrast, her cousin Mike brings things to his office with reckless abandon because he doesn't give a moment's thought to where these new additions will be stored. When clutter accumulates, he blames himself for not being a neat person. But even Claire could not function in an office with inadequate storage space. Nor would she try. She would do whatever necessary to obtain the storage tools she needed.

  Quick Fix: Create a place for three to five items that are chronically out on your desk. Keep them in their newly created home for right now. Later, we'll help you assess more permanent solutions, such as more drawers, shelves, and nooks.

- **Fear of forgetfulness.** Ever leave things in view so you won't forget them? You're not alone. Leaving items out because we're afraid we'll forget about them is a common way forgetful people "visually cue" themselves to stay on task.

  Quick Fix: Sidestep the memory issue by composing a project list to jog your memory about what you need to do—and tack it where it will always be in view. Neatly label containers, drawers, shelves, files, and boxes to remind you where things go.

- **Assembly-line thinking.** Rather than putting away papers, projects, file folders, and other supplies as they're used, some people prefer to designate a time to put everything away at once. It seems more efficient to them, even though they see their neighbors in neater offices quickly return items to storage. While they wait for that designated "put away" time to come, if it ever does, their office mess mushrooms. "Stow as you go" is not a motto for them, and it shows.

Quick Fix: Resist the urge to keep things out until a big cleanup time. Instead, commit to putting things back in place in a timely manner for one day. Evaluate how that works for you, and commit to making it a permanent habit. On occasion it's appropriate to stack materials so they can be handled all at once, such as collecting patients' files to be returned as a group to the storage room for filing. But other than in these special cases, avoid assembly-line thinking.

- **Enjoyment of happy happenstances.** Sometimes good things are unearthed in clutter. Finding an uncashed check just when you need it or stumbling across a warm note from a colleague who has moved on can make dealing with clutter a little like opening a present. These phenomena temporarily defang the pain clutter causes, and for a time may even make it seem desirable. But over the long-term, clutter is debilitating and will negatively affect your work, your mental energy, and your personal satisfaction.

  Quick Fix: Don't let an occasional happy happenstance convince you to keep clutter around. Put things in their correct places and know where your things are. When you do that, entering your office will become a happy happenstance you can count on.

- **Distractibility.** Distractions can be like punches, and being able to roll with them is an enviable strength. Phone calls, emails, people stopping in to talk, spontaneous meetings—all can pull us from the task at hand. Sometimes we lure ourselves away from important activities by taking a bathroom break, having a snack, or moving on to a more pleasant task. We like distractions because our attention span is short and we like variety. But distractions can take over. It's always more difficult to take up where we left off than to keep going while we're in the groove. A lot of half-done jobs lie around the office and nag at us—often in the form of (you guessed it!) clutter.

Quick Fix: Commit to staying on task for a period of time—then set a timer to hold you accountable. Close your office door and post a sign letting would-be interrupters know you're not available. If you can't shut out distractions at your regular workspace, escape to a library or conference room until the task is done. If that's not an option, try turning your chair so your back is facing the entrance to your space.

- **Indecision.** Many perfectionists masquerade as disorganized people. Because of our high standards, we fear making wrong decisions. So, rather than do the hard thing of, say, deciding how to handle a paper that's neither obviously necessary nor obviously trash, we place it in a pile "just for now" and move on to something easier. The "just for now" pile grows, creating a clutter mountain.

  Judith Kolberg, a veteran professional organizer, suggests the following game to break decision roadblocks like this: look at items in a personal way. Some papers are "friends" that we keep for sure. Some are "strangers" that are useless and easier to ditch. "Acquaintances" are the hard ones about which we vacillate.[1]

  Quick Fix: Set up an in-box labeled "Undecided" to hold the "acquaintances," and keep them from creeping into existing piles. Then take ten minutes at the end of the day to decide about each one. Still can't decide on some? Return them to the box for the next decision session.

Eventually many will disqualify themselves with age or will resolve themselves without needing our decision.

- **Playing the part.** Sometimes the clutterer may play the part of "the messy guy" at the office. The butt of friendly jokes, he goes along with the gentle ribbing, even posting signs with little jabs of his own over his debris-laden desk, such as "A clean desk is the sign of a sick mind." Secretly, he tells himself, *I'd like to get organized. But what if I try, and I can't make it stick? I'll just expose myself to more ridicule!* Fear keeps him from trying to change.

  Quick Fix: Resolve to be brave! Feel the fear and follow the steps in this book anyway. A determined effort to improve, coupled with a few new habits, will bring success. You're going to love the new, organized you!

- **Poor time management.** We all know it happens. Time slips up on us. Studies show that disorganized people have a poorer sense of the movement of time than organized people. That often means we don't manage our work schedule well. All of a sudden, we notice we have to go to a meeting, and up we jump—leaving unfinished work behind. The mess mounts.

  Quick Fix: Commit to using a planner and make sure every event is recorded. Note the time of each meeting, and above it, the time you need to *leave* for that meeting. Soon you'll begin to respond subconsciously to the earlier time. Just feeling less rushed will help your organizational efforts immensely.

Other Common Clutter Causes

Stress

Stress is not always bad. A little stress can be helpful. When your on-the-job stress occurs—such as an alert that your boss or an important client is coming to your office—you shift into high gear and do a remarkable job of clearing out clutter in a short period of time.

But there comes a point when stress is not helpful. Too much stress over a long period of time begins to affect productivity—and your quality of life.

A chronically messy office causes stress. At the same time, being under stress can hinder your ability to organize. Talk about a vicious cycle!

Here's a solution: When you're feeling stressed, stop and take a break. Stretch. Sometimes stepping away from the issue will help you gain perspective. Your physical and mental energy will be refreshed and you will tackle the job with renewed vigor.

Fatigue

Maybe fatigue is what's holding you back in your attempts to get organized. This is a factor that requires immediate and serious attention. Some causes of fatigue are medical, such as anemia, low thyroid, depression, or other physical factors.

The main cause of fatigue in the workplace can be blamed on overwork triggered by poor time management, failure to delegate, too many tasks, or a too-hectic lifestyle. Tiredness may also be caused by boredom or poor sleep habits. Add in poor eating habits, too much caffeine, and too little exercise and you've got a recipe for one tired individual.

Regardless of the cause, the feeling of physical powerlessness affects both your daily living and your ability to function successfully at work—especially when it comes to taking on the new project of getting organized.

Take fatigue seriously. Don't stop until you find its root causes, then address them. Follow through until you are able to function to your fullest capacity. When you have found the energy you need, you will be ready to make the progress you want.

Attention Deficit Disorder

Everybody has occasions when they forget something or neglect to do something. They say to themselves, "That was so scatterbrained!" A little of this is normal. But there comes a time when it signals a more significant problem such as Attention Deficit Disorder (ADD).

Years ago, no one had ever heard of adult Attention Deficit Disorder. But now, its acceptance as a real condition has offered an explanation for formerly unexplainable behavior and inattention. In his book *Crazy Busy*, psychiatrist Edward Hallowell, MD, describes the symptoms of a person with untreated ADD. If you think you could be suffering from this clutter-causing condition, it's worth checking out.

Gina fit the description perfectly. She was a thirty-seven-year-old manager in a large company. Fun and full of energy, she oversaw the work of people in cubicles. She was excellent in her chosen field of advertising because she was wonderfully creative and consistently hit the nail on the head in advertising campaigns. Because she was warm and enthusiastic, she made a great presentation to clients. They asked for her by name.

But when it came to the nitty-gritty of getting things done, she rushed around a lot, feeling impatient wherever she was, and getting frustrated easily. Sometimes Gina lost focus in the middle of a task or a conversation because some other thought caught her attention. She struggled to pay attention to any one issue for more than a short time.

Because she was so creative, she was put in charge of many projects. But at times she failed to complete what she was doing because she had so many projects going simultaneously. Her attention hopped from one to another.

Frequently, Gina felt her brain was overloaded. The piles of stuff that surrounded her in her cluttered office made her feel powerless, and she resolved each day to do a better job of keeping her office neat.

People who suffer from true ADD usually can bring the chaos they experience under control by making behavioral changes, using a planner, keeping surfaces clear, setting timers, implementing new habits, making lists, and finding other techniques that help them stay focused. In his book *ADD Success Stories*, Tom Hartmann summarizes it this way: "People with ADD are often disorganized and cluttered, and can benefit tremendously from learning organizational strategies that teach them how to impose order and systems on their schooling and work."[2]

Whether you truly have ADD or you just haven't learned the tricks to staying organized, the techniques we'll teach you in this book will help you feel more in control of your surroundings—and look more in control too!

Modern Life

In the mid-1990s, Dr. Hallowell noticed that he was beginning to have a lot of patients who had ADD-like symptoms but didn't have true ADD. His final conclusion was that they suffered from a severe case of "modern life."

Contemporary life has been getting busier for decades. But Dr. Hallowell surmised that the pace of life had been ratcheted up so much by modern technology it had reached an unhealthy crescendo. People were becoming forgetful and unfocused as they went about their hectic lives. Many were so disturbed about distraction problems they were seeking professional help.

Dr. Hallowell observed that in today's world we try to own too much, accomplish too much, tune in to too much, watch too much, and know too much. We've learned to take pleasure in the hectic pace. We seek out more because we enjoy the stimulation, the adrenaline rush, and the power we feel when we are in the midst of overload.

In all the excitement, the home or corporate office falls victim. It naturally becomes overlooked and under-maintained. Dr. Hallowell suggests that the first step to recovery is to recognize our limitations and select only a few things to which we dedicate our time and energy.[3]

If your office and your work truly are important to you, you may need to scale back on other activities that steal your attention and energy. Then you may find you have the focus you need to get your office organized so it can support your efforts rather than drag you down.

Take some time to think. Ask yourself, "Could I have true ADD that needs professional help? Or am I suffering from a severe case of modern life?" Both require action: thoughtful consideration, deliberate scaling back, and some hard decision making on how to prioritize your time.

If I'm So Smart, Why Haven't I Already Gotten Organized?

The term "executive function" refers to how we execute the jobs we have to do. A person with good executive function works efficiently toward his or her goal of getting organized and staying organized. For some, that comes naturally. Others struggle with setting and accomplishing goals.

Like so many other organizing skills, executive function does not reflect on a person's intelligence. Many an absent-minded professor or brilliant scientist is known for a disheveled appearance and a cluttered office. Nobody knows for sure why some of us are good at executive function and others are not. As in sports, natural ability is involved, but it's not the only factor.

Whatever the reasons for our challenges with executive function, we can set up ways to overcome them. But first we have to identify what's throwing executive function off track. It could be:

- **Poor working memory.** In doing any complex work, it's necessary to hold several parts of the procedure in mind simultaneously. And that calls for a strong "working memory," also known as short-term memory. Some of us are low-functioning when it comes to working memory. That can make even a simple activity difficult. Add on distractions and Attention Deficit Disorder, and a small memory problem can lead to serious problems staying on task.

If you struggle to complete projects, your working memory could be the culprit. But you can work around the problem by simply keeping a running log of notes consistently in one place, such as a notebook or legal pad, as you progress through tasks. The writing will help emphasize what you need to remember, and checking your notes periodically will keep you on track. It may also help to keep a "Random Information" notebook where you can store tidbits you don't want to forget. We'll address this in detail later, along with other specific strategies for organizing your office.

- **Lack of visual alertness.** Efficient people quickly notice when things are out of place. They know where their materials are, and they aren't able to work as well if things are out of order. However, disorganized people work with less distress in a messy office because they really don't notice how bad the clutter looks. They tune in to clutter only when it's called to their attention, sometimes by a visit from a boss or client. Sometimes it's by way of a note ("Please remove the clutter so the cleaning crew can work!") or an overheard comment ("How can he work in that mess?").

  This lack of visual alertness can often be blamed on what is sometimes called a "figure/ground problem." That's just a poor ability to notice the figures (things like clutter) that are in the background (floor, desk, shelves). People who struggle with this are actually surprised on a regular basis to realize they've left items out. They have to consciously rally their visual attention in order to zero in on what needs to be put away.

If you're lacking in visual alertness, schedule time every now and then to stop and pay attention to your surroundings. Sometimes just directing your focus helps you notice what needs to be done to keep clutter from piling up. Curl your hand into a circle and hold it over one eye, then shut the other. Peer through your "spyglass." Scan the area. If the clutter's piled up, use the strategies in this book to get it under control.

- **Slipups in sequencing.** Sequencing is managing the steps of an activity. The goal: use sequencing to complete tasks in the most logical and efficient way. Sounds obvious. But as with many organizing skills, it comes easily to some and not to others.

Scientists have coined the terms of "left brain" and "right brain" to compare these differences in thinking. Most organizing tasks are best accomplished with a sequential approach. Knowing the series of steps to take and following them in order is the best way to get an office under control and keep it organized. Left-brain thinkers often do well at this, even when they don't take a lot of time to plan. They often tend to be naturally organized anyway.

Right-brain thinkers try to tackle the job of organizing without much thought, working in a random way that, in the end, isn't very effective. They'll benefit from setting up a plan for how to begin and then how to proceed. If you're a right-brain thinker with a disorganized office, jot down, in any order, the tasks you know you need to tackle to get organized. If you don't have a clue about where to start, don't worry. We'll tell you the steps. If you have some ideas, list them in a sequence that makes sense to you. Writing them down will bring clarity. Later, as you work, you can evaluate and rearrange the steps. Any planning is better than none, and will help you clarify the steps you need to take to organize your office—even if you're not a natural planner.

- **Failure to plan ahead.** A person with well-honed organizational skills may be working on step five of a project, for instance, with an idea of how it will affect step twelve down the line. He or she will make adjustments accordingly to be prepared for step twelve when it arrives.

A person who lacks strong planning skills may not efficiently prepare for future steps. That can be a barrier to staying organized. If you often fail to plan properly, you probably have a hopeful attitude that things will work out when you get to future steps, but you're usually disappointed. That's not surprising. Order seldom happens on its own. You may forge ahead anyway, knowing it would have been so much easier if you'd planned better from the beginning. We'll help you plan your attack for getting organized and staying that way.

All of these characteristics can hold us back in our efforts to get organized. But they're often difficult for us to recognize in ourselves. For instance, many struggling with disorganization simply dismiss or overlook executive function as a factor. Instead, they fret about the problems that result from their disorganization, frequently vowing, "I just have to work harder." They avoid organizing projects because they haven't really identified the cause of their chronic struggle, and therefore they've never really found an approach that works in helping them stay organized. They believe they could get organized—if they found the time to attack the problem. But somehow, that never happens.

Learning the skills to get organized and stay that way can dramatically affect our quality of life. A more organized life is a more productive and satisfying life. Just becoming aware of the issues that may be holding you back is a giant step forward in helping you address them.

When You *Know* You're Not to Blame

Maybe the clutter really isn't your fault. You just need to know how to get it under control. The recipe for success is in the pages that follow. But to get started now, use these tips to attack:

- **Colleague clutter.** Occasionally, the person perceived to be a clutterer is not primarily responsible for the clutter. He or she shares an office with a true clutterer or is in circumstances that make it almost impossible to maintain a neat environment.
  Quick fix: Set boundaries. Don't let others' clutter get on your desk or in your space. Move it physically back where it belongs, even if it means putting it in the owner's chair.
- **A newly expanded workload.** Downsizing and "rightsizing" can result in an increase in additional responsibilities that used to belong to others, and that can cause an explosion of disorganization in the office.
  Quick fix: Be realistic. Understand there is only so much you can do. Prioritize and focus on the most important things. Ask for help if you need it. And commit to employing the organizing skills you'll learn in the following chapters. They'll help a lot!
- **A super-busy office.** In offices with a large staff, there's a constant push of activity with many things happening simultaneously. Workers hop from task to task without time to transition smoothly from one activity to the next. Out-of-place items pile up as workers scurry.
  Quick fix: If you have a naturally neat colleague who's willing, offer to take on one of her tasks so she can set aside time to tidy up common areas at regular intervals. Leaving the office in order at the end of the day will help everyone get started on the right track the next morning.

Picture your office organized. Visualize the outcome vividly, then write a list of the steps you can see at this point. (We'll tell you the rest later.) Start a list of materials you know you'll need. Share your goals with a friend or a colleague. You're on your way!

The problem of disorganization *can* be conquered. But you have to begin the work by facing your own personal characteristics. It's the only way to make true progress. We know you can do it with the information, motivation, and inspiration you'll find in this book.

Starting on page 207, we've created a section to guide you in the specific changes you need to make. Read the questions and tasks at the end of each chapter, then flip to chapter 20, "Smart and Useful Ideas," to write your answers. As you move ahead in your organizing, use this chapter to keep focused on the job at hand.

Start by making just one change. Move on from there. Every step is progress!

Smart Steps in the Right Direction

Flip now to chapter 20, "Smart and Useful Ideas," beginning on page 207, to continue creating a powerful tool that can help you stay on track in your organizing by answering these questions:

1.1. Of the reasons for clutter listed above, which one rings your bell the loudest?

1.2. What can you do to minimize that characteristic's impact on your organizing efforts?

1.3. Which quick fixes will you employ now to make an immediate difference in your office?

Mini-Quiz

1. Do you set high—sometimes unrealistic—standards?

2. Do you use techniques to overcome procrastination?

3. Are you willing to take some baby steps out of the morass of disorganization?

Now we are heading into deep waters. A "yes" to numbers 1 and 3, and a "no" to number 2, means this next chapter can help you steer clear of wrecking on the shoals of disorder.

2

Help! I'm Sinking My Own Ship

We have met the enemy and he is us.

Pogo comic strip (Walt Kelly)

Striving for perfection is the greatest stopper there is. It's your excuse to yourself for not doing anything. Instead, strive for excellence, doing your best.

Sir Laurence Olivier

Action Highlights

By the end of this chapter, you'll be prepared to:

- Address approaches that hold you back.
- Make changes in your behavior that will liberate you.
- Challenge the urge to save too much.
- Avoid debilitating time-wasters.

None of us set out to sink our own ship. But many of us tolerate unproductive ways of thinking and acting that do it for us: perfectionism, procrastination, and saving too much stuff. If we're to move forward in any endeavor, we have to patch these holes in our boat.

When we get control of these areas, a lot of the weight that causes us to ride low in the water will be thrown overboard, sending us into calmer seas with smoother sailing.

Toxic Perfectionism

Many messy offices stay that way because the person responsible for the mess won't start an organization project until the job can be done perfectly. The result is an office that's anything but perfect.

There are two kinds of perfectionism. One is characterized by a desire for excellence and the enjoyment that comes from striving for quality. This, of course, is normal and good. Go for it!

Toxic perfectionism is another story. It's an extreme condition that prevents some people from feeling satisfaction in their work. In their eyes, nothing is ever done well enough. They strain compulsively and unremittingly toward impossible goals, and measure their worth by an unrealistic standard they never can meet.

In organizing projects, we see this trait rear its ugly head in this way: a person spends so much time on unimportant details that the project grinds to a halt under the sheer weight of its complexity.

Toxic perfectionism is spurred on by a number of reasons: fear of making a mistake or a wrong decision, perception of parental standards, or personal standards. Whatever the reason, it keeps us from reaching our goals.

Some jobs, like performing brain surgery or piloting a plane, call for a high degree of attention to detail. And even these jobs can't be done perfectly all the time.

Most jobs don't require this kind of focus on details. Office organizing is one of those tasks that doesn't have to be perfect. It just has to be done. There's a motto in that: "Better done than perfect."

If you like things to be right and you strive for excellence, that's good—as long as it's under control. If you are paralyzed and won't even begin an organizing task for fear you won't have the time, energy, or ability to do it perfectly, you are moving in the direction of neurotic perfectionism.

What should you do if you're the type who waits to start a job until you can do it perfectly or until you know you can finish it completely in an unreasonable amount of time? Or if you keep projects at 90 percent for years and years because you're afraid that the finished project will not be good enough?

It's simple. Decide to fight back. Commit to take on the project of organizing your office. Challenge those unrealistic attitudes that are crippling you. Don't base your sense of self-worth on your performance. Face the fear of not living up to your own standards—then live anyway!

Follow the steps in this book. Then call in someone you trust to tell you when your project is good enough—and really trust that judgment.

Try lowering your standards for just one project so you can get used to the feeling. Instead of cornering yourself with the idea that your office must look good enough to be on the cover of a magazine, consider just revamping it so that it helps you do your job more efficiently. Instead of avoiding the project until you can make it fabulous, take it on, pledging to celebrate when it's a pleasant, orderly place to work.

Doing this will help you begin to break a deeply ingrained habit. You can always go back and improve the organizing project later—maybe later you'll be able to upgrade from plastic storage boxes to something classier. But allow yourself to feel good about simply getting this important task done in a timely fashion.

One of our favorite sayings to challenge perfectionist thinking is: "If it's worth doing at all, it's worth doing poorly."

Sure, we're kidding a bit. But if perfectionism is keeping you from getting your office organized, perhaps you should take a deep breath and plunge in, repeating as you work: "Better done than perfect. Better done than perfect."

Sabotaged by Saving

Perfectionism can lead to another obstacle in your quest for an office that remains organized: a bent for saving.

Barry was one of those with an overstuffed office due to excessive saving. He thought it was perfectly reasonable to keep anything that could entertain or benefit other people. Scattered around his office were jokes and cartoons, clippings of interesting articles, pictures, postcards, funny stories, and magazines that often related to someone else's work.

He saw himself as a kind of unofficial librarian, except that nothing was cataloged. So he was rarely successful in passing along the nuggets he'd collected. As a result, the ever-growing pile spilled off his desk onto every available surface in his office.

He also kept a variety of supplies, in the event someone might have a need. And, though he wouldn't have guessed it, his officemates hardly appreciated his efforts to be helpful and friendly. Annoyed by the growing mess, they avoided allowing him to foist unwanted items on them.

Barry saved things for himself too. Being frugal, he bought bargains and accepted castoffs, whether he had a need for them or not. He saw value in almost everything. Any colleague's trash was Barry's treasure.

Fear of making the wrong decision about what to keep causes the saver to turn off good decision-making skills and switch into do-not-discard mode. This is a case where perfectionism causes paralysis. And the result is too many unnecessary things in an office too small to contain them.

If you save too many things you'll probably never use, try these strategies:

- **Let go** of things that have no reasonable and foreseeable use or intended recipient.
- **Deliver** the things you're keeping for someone else. Only hold on to what you need.
- **Bravely face the fear** of discarding something of questionable value, and do it anyway. Having the space and order you are positive you need is worth the gamble.

Put Off Procrastinating!

We all have too much to do. But do we really need to do it all to be successful? Maybe not.

In 1897, Italian economist Vilfredo Pareto noticed that 80 percent of Italy's wealth belonged to 20 percent of the population. What's now known as the Pareto Principle—or the 80/20 Rule—is useful in understanding productivity trends in many areas of life. Basically, it suggests that 80 percent of the results in any endeavor come from 20 percent of the effort.

We see this principle in action all around us. For example, consider the school administrator, who spends 80 percent of her time dealing with 20 percent of the students. It's said that 80 percent of sales comes from 20 percent of customers.

In your office, you'd probably agree that 80 percent of what's filed is never looked at again. And by tackling 20 percent of your tasks, you can generate 80 percent of the benefit of doing the whole job. In other words, we need to train ourselves to major on the majors.

Now comes the hard part—pinpointing the most important 20 percent. When we languish in indecision, we tend to procrastinate doing important jobs and waste time on unimportant activities. Maybe this is what's kept you from the important task of getting your office in shape?

Ah, if only we could decide on the 20 percent that's most important, then do it in a timely fashion. Just think of it! Our lives would be so much easier and more productive. Less stress, more productivity, more discretionary time, and fewer crises!

There is a belief among Japanese businessmen that repeated crises are the result of poor business management. Much of that poor management involves putting off what needs to be done. Putting off important things eventually gums up our progress. To use another metaphor, procrastinating is the worm that eats the heart out of our success, without our even being aware until it is too late. Failure to organize activities well will definitely create a crisis—one of clutter and disorganization.

Like few other things, procrastination is directly related to our emotions and our energy level. American psychologist and philosopher William James said that "nothing is so fatiguing as the eternal hanging on of uncompleted tasks."

And nothing is so satisfying and energizing as finally accomplishing a task that has been hanging over our heads.

Janine was handling papers in her office when she came across a quote by Pablo Picasso that she'd torn from a newspaper: "Only put off until tomorrow what you are willing to die having left undone."

Morbid! she thought. But it rang a bell as she looked at her disorganized, cluttered office. She asked herself, *If I were gone and others were going though my things, would I want them to find that I had not dealt with this mess—and they would have to do it instead?*

Somehow, this was her turning point in how seriously she took her office-organizing project. She immediately set in motion a process to hold herself accountable so she couldn't put off the job any longer.

She posted a note on a social networking website, alerting friends that she'd be working on the project for six hours the next day. She even challenged others to join her in similar tasks of their own at the same time.

That made it official. Now there was no turning back. To her, making her plans public and promising to post a report later made her feel like she now had a drill sergeant standing over her, barking orders and warning her not to quit until the task was complete.

Now, she does this whenever she has a task that tempts her to procrastinate. "I enjoy it," she says, beaming. "And I've gotten much more accomplished."

Why We Procrastinate

We've seen how perfectionism can cause procrastination and discourage us from taking on a job until we're sure we can do it with an unreasonably high level of quality.

Boredom can also be the culprit. Sometimes we think we just can't bear the tedium of certain jobs. Most creative types don't like the monotony of keeping things organized. And let's face it—most of the organizing process is not a hoot.

But staying organized often opens the door to more creativity. Many a wonderful, creative project has been derailed because creative genius gets lost in a muddle of messiness.

Recognizing how much she resisted uninspiring tasks, Ria confronted herself with this realization: "One puzzling aspect of the I-don't-do-boring attitude is that, once I complete a long-delayed task, I often marvel at how easy it was, especially compared with the anxiety and inconvenience of putting it off. I feel a sense of elation at the results, or at simply getting it behind me."

"So," she asked herself, "why is it so hard to muster a sense of motivation, when I've had such positive feelings come from completing long-put-off tasks?"

We'd all do well to ask ourselves this question when it comes to doing the nitty-gritty of office organizing. We will be so very happy when it's done! So why do we put it off?

- **Learned helplessness.** Maybe you've tried your best to get organized, either in your office or elsewhere. It hasn't worked, and you don't know why. Now you've given up trying. Oh, maybe not entirely. But your can-do attitude has taken a big hit, and you find it hard to rally your forces to try again. You've accepted failure, or at least inaction, as a reasonable option. It's not. We're going to give you the tools to make this time a success.

- **Blame game.** We may procrastinate in order to wait for a roadblock to disappear. Sometimes that's a legitimate delay, such as when we have to wait for a decision from someone else before moving forward. In other cases, we probably could have or should have anticipated the problem and headed it off in the first place. If you're procrastinating, focus on what's detaining you and concentrate on removing that roadblock. Ask yourself, "Is there a specific issue that gets in the way of creating my ideal office?"

- **Zapped mental energy.** When we hate to do a job, we wait until some kind of deadline is upon us and ride the adrenaline wave of panic to get it done. But research shows that work done under this kind of pressure is usually inferior to work that is well planned. It is time to set a date and start getting your office into shape. You'll be amazed at the energy that will come from that!

- **Rebellion.** Anger at the person who requires you to do a job can cause you to procrastinate. *I'll show her—I just won't do it*, you may subconsciously be telling yourself. That makes procrastination a perfect form of passive resistance. Sometimes we even refuse to do something in our best interest because of an experience in the past we're still trying to resolve. Maybe you were bugged about keeping things neat as a kid, so now you're rebelling. Time to get over that and allow yourself the luxury of a well-organized office.

- **Busyness.** If you have too much on your plate, some things are bound to fall off. Too many tasks means some will never get done, or they'll get done later than they should. In today's world, being too busy and careening between an overabundance of activities that force themselves on us keep us from giving time to what's important. In short, we procrastinate and fail to do the good stuff, because we simply run out of time.
- **Fear of failure.** How many books remain unwritten because the would-be writer is afraid to try? For some, it's better to have a wonderful book "in my head" than to put it on paper and find that it's not nearly as good in plain old black-and-white. Besides, then others can see it and might even criticize it—a good reason to put off the job forever. Right? Wrong.
- **The job's too hard.** Sometimes, a job simply seems insurmountable. We give up before we even start. Not much potential for progress with that plan.

How many good businesses have died in embryo form because the creator was afraid to move ahead? If you set up your office, will others expect more of you than you think you can deliver? Don't let that stop you! You can do it! Identify the issues holding *you* back. It's the first step in challenging their hold on your thinking.

Get Moving

You know you need to get organized. So yank the rug out from under your habit of procrastinating.

- **Write down the task you need to do.** Clarifying it in words demystifies it.
- **Promise yourself a reward** for doing something that has stymied you.

- **Vow to yourself and another person** that you'll take a specific step toward accomplishing the task, suggests psychologist Albert Ellis. Commit to a consequence if it's not done by the deadline you set. For example, "If I don't get this bill in the mail by noon, I will leave a twenty dollar tip for the server at lunch."
- **Get started on an easy part** of the project rather than tackling it head-on.
- **Ask for help.** Then set a time to work with a partner on the project.
- **Set a timer** for fifteen minutes and do a little at a time.
- **Use the "Swiss cheese" method** of author Alan Laiken.[4] "Poke holes" in the project a little at a time by taking small steps. Buy file folders. Look up a piece of furniture on the internet. Sometimes one step that takes just five minutes can be the breakthrough you need.

Now, post a picture or written description of your goal. Break the project into baby steps. Toddle forward. Baby steps. Baby steps.

If you follow the steps described in this book one by one, you'll see change. And quickly.

We've addressed personal hang-ups that could be holding you back. Soon you'll consider the stories of people who've been where you are. Find out how they overcame clutter and "dissed" disorganization. Live their successes with them and soon you'll be the one celebrating triumph.

Smart Steps in the Right Direction

Flip now to chapter 20, "Smart and Useful Ideas," beginning on page 207, to continue creating a powerful tool that can help you stay on track in your organizing by answering these questions:

2.1. Which behaviors interfere with your organizing goals?

2.2. What do you plan to do to overcome them?

2.3. What can you do this week to improve your organization at the office?

Mini-Quiz

1. Are you ready to move forward in getting organized?

2. Do you have an organizational goal clearly in mind?

3. Do you know exactly what you need to have to get where you want to go?

A "yes" to the first question and "no" to the others is an invitation to read the next encouraging chapter.

3

Not Brain Surgery . . . but Close

Vision without action is merely a dream. Action without vision just passes the time. Vision with action can change the world.

Ralph Waldo Emerson

Action Highlights

By the end of this chapter, you'll be prepared to:

- Realize the significance of your office.
- Commit to begin with baby steps.
- Remember the big picture.

Creating and maintaining an office that both looks good and works well definitely isn't as difficult as performing brain surgery. But for many of us who seem to have come up short in the distribution of organizing genes, it feels like it is.

I Don't Want to Be Disorganized Anymore Because . . .

- People think it means I'm not capable.
- I lose time I need for productive activities by looking for important papers, key information, and other missing items.
- My lack of efficiency costs the company money—and often forces me to duplicate efforts.
- I can't escape the nagging, even depressing, feeling that I should get this under control.
- Stress, stress, stress!

I Want to Be Well-Organized Because . . .

- I'd accomplish so much more in less time (and I could spend more time with family and friends).
- I could make more money.
- My work would be so much easier and more pleasant.
- My boss would be happier about the way I use my time.
- Colleagues and clients would be more confident in my ability.
- More balance in my life. Less stress!

The truth is it's not complicated. It's actually pretty simple. In short, it's nothing like brain surgery.

But it is important. Very important. Your office is your partner in success. Take care of it, and it will take care of you.

Ready to start? Good. Take a deep breath and close your eyes. That's right, close 'em. Now, what would your office be like if it were perfect? Imagine it. Dream it. Dream big. Very, very big.

See the furniture. The gleaming, uncluttered surfaces. Tools and supplies neatly stowed where they're easy to find and within reach. Decorative items that add beauty and inspiration.

Do you see it? Is it everything you want in an office? If not, try again. Only a big dream like that will motivate you to make a change.

The D.O. (Doctor of Organization) Diagnoses His Patients

- **Pilomania.** The uncontrollable urge to stack papers for future reference.
- **Filophobia.** The fear of putting anything into the dark recesses of a filing cabinet.
- **L-ADD.** Lack of Attention to Desk Disorder.
- **Justincaser.** Keeps, but can't locate, things that will never be needed again.
- **Decisionalysis.** Paralysis of the decision-making ability of an individual.
- **Clutterholic.** Compulsively creates chaos in well-ordered areas.
- **Shelf Denial.** Avoidance of acquiring enough shelving to hold the necessary equipment, resulting in the use of floor space as one large flat shelf.
- **Project Management Hallucinosis.** The erroneous belief that one must wait for just the right humor in order to tackle a project, rather than facing the reality that organized people respond to the need, not the mood.
- **Starter Stutter.** Finding it hard to get started, getting hung up at the beginning of a project.
- **Bipolar Dis-Ordered.** Roller-coaster method of organizing (clean up, spiral down into disorder, clean up, spiral down into disorder, feel sick).
- **Infoholic.** Addicted to the gathering of information from newspapers, magazines, books, television, and internet sources in the form of clippings, notebook jottings, computer files, or deep storage in the old cerebrum.
- **Don't-Finish-Up Fever.** Tendency to leave an activity before it's fully finished or before materials and tools are returned to their proper storage areas.
- **Distractophelia.** Condition of repeatedly losing focus in the middle of a thought or action, resulting in a trail of started-but-unfinished activities.

Now we can begin the transformation with consistent, incremental changes. Baby steps.

But first: a reminder. You've been put on this earth at this time for an important purpose. Be sure not to just muddle through the God-given design for your life.

Much of your productivity depends on the condition of your office. Significant things with far-reaching consequences happen there every day.

Your office is the stage on which you live out an important part of your life. Set that stage for your best performance and when the curtain rises every day, you will be ready.

Some day, like us, you hope to hear, "Well done, good and faithful servant" (see Matt. 5:21). Then you'll realize what you knew on some level all the time: this space wasn't really just an office. It was so much more.

Smart Steps in the Right Direction

Flip now to chapter 20, "Smart and Useful Ideas," beginning on page 207, to continue creating a powerful tool that can help you stay on track in your organizing by answering these questions:

3.1. Flesh out that dream. Write a description of your perfect office. See, feel, and smell the sights of exposed surfaces and within storage areas such as filing cabinets and drawers. Most importantly, write out the driving force of why you care so much, and how you will feel when you reach your goal. Supercharge your dream with emotion. When that's finished and nobody's looking, do a happy dance in the midst of the order and beauty you have created.

3.2. Which of the disease symptoms above would you report on your visit to the doctor of organization? (You can report more than one.)

Mini-Quiz

1. Have you looked at your office recently with an objective eye, as a visitor would?

2. Can you muster enthusiasm for creating the kind of office you want?

3. Are you willing to put out some time, energy, and money to make important changes to your office?

If you answered "no" to number 1, and "yes" to numbers 2 and 3, you'll see major progress by the end of the next chapter. Enjoy!

4

Assess the Mess

Start by doing what's necessary, then do what's possible, and suddenly you are doing the impossible.

St. Francis of Assisi

Action Highlights

By the end of this chapter, you'll be prepared to:

- Name one good thing about your office.
- Clarify necessary changes by writing your ideas.
- Decide on specific changes you can make to start improving your space.

Organizing a chaotic office is an unpleasant and even scary job. For many, it rivals getting a root canal or a colonoscopy—necessary, but put off for as long as possible.

You know you should be courageous about tackling the office but it is so much easier to avoid it, even if that means living under a cloud of nagging procrastination. Even if you battle confusion, struggling to function in an office that doesn't work for you, you excuse your neglect by saying, "I don't have time right now. I'm just way too busy."

Eventually, the pain in your tooth or the worry about your health overcomes your reluctance—and to the doctor or dentist you go. It's the same way with a disorganized office that makes your job—and maybe even your entire life—a whole lot more unpleasant than it has to be.

When you finally decide it's easier to take action than to delay further, a huge weight lifts from your shoulders. When a task you've been dreading is done, you feel like doing a happy dance and scold yourself, wondering *Why didn't I do that sooner?*

You know you can't afford to keep putting off this "good medicine." The gnawing worry of disorganization has been on your mind for a long time, and you've decided to pause long enough to do something about it. That's why you're reading this book.

You're ready to do the deed. The hour has come!

And this time you're not alone. You have two supporters who will lead you through the process and stick with you every step of the way. At the end, you'll cheer your success and take us both out to lunch to celebrate.

Well, maybe you'll take two other friends out to lunch in our places, but it will be a celebration, nonetheless.

Open the Office Door (You Can Do It!)

As you stand on the threshold of your office, negative thoughts flood you. At this point, men often react with angry frustration. They might turn and walk out, or blame someone else for the mess. Most often, they stuff their feelings and resolve to keep plowing doggedly forward with their work.

Women will often feel depressed, overwhelmed, out-of-control, and generally helpless. It doesn't get more negative than that!

The first thing you need to do is turn your thinking around. Introduce positive thoughts into this whole ordeal. Berating yourself for past failures doesn't help. Instead, as you gaze into your office, tell yourself something true and uplifting. Everybody has at least one positive thing he or she can say, such as:

- At least I know where most things are.
- In spite of how my office looks, my business is thriving.
- I'm very good with returning phone calls.
- I just completed a big project well.
- I have a good "morning system," and I'm always on time for work.
- I keep up with finances well.
- Even though it appears to be in disarray, there are some systems in place that work pretty well.

Another positive: you're reading this book. You have already taken the first step toward change.

To help you keep walking forward, we've included lots of anecdotes about real people, whose names have been changed, of course. You will be comforted, encouraged, and inspired to make the changes you need. Let's step into Doreen's story, as she took those first steps toward order in her office.

Doreen's Mission: Bring This Office under Control!

Doreen worked for a mission organization. Because she was often gone on mission trips for months at a time, each time she returned she faced a looming mountain of unsorted mail.

Her fellow missionaries, who shared space around her, placed both her business mail and her personal mail together on her desk, chairs, countertop, and the floor, as she'd asked.

And there it all lay, awaiting her return—growing into a threatening paper monster that gobbled up her enthusiasm for coming home.

Each time she entered her office after an absence, her spirit slumped in despair as she looked at the daunting job before her. Pressure mounted. People were waiting for replies, bills were late, junk mail was mixed in with important papers, and it was almost impossible to decide which items needed to be addressed first without tearing open every piece of mail and reading it.

"At least I don't have to be in this office every day," she consoled herself. "This is the price I pay for a great job."

But the reality was that she seemed to be the only person in the organization with such an issue with paper clutter. Others took trips, came back, and dispatched their mail much more quickly than she did. Her traveling companion was back in business shortly after they returned. "You've really got a job here," she commented to Doreen as she passed down the hall. "Something's got to change!" Doreen muttered, plunking down onto her swivel chair.

If things were perfect, she thought, *I would have one place where the mail could be neatly collected, instead of just dumped all over in piles. I would have a shelf to hold books that are now stacked on floors and tables—and it could collect any that come in the mail while I'm away. I'd have filing cabinets in my office, instead of sharing one in the front office. I'd have a filing system that works. I would even have a curio cabinet for the things I bring back from the mission fields.*

Suddenly encouraged, she began furiously listing her ideas on a legal pad. As she wrote, her ideas became clearer. Hope spilled from her pen. Beside each item on her list she drew a tiny box where she'd make a check after the step was accomplished. Now, what had seemed impossible looked doable. Yes! Of course it was! She could do this thing!

Doreen suddenly felt a huge sense of relief. Even though she'd begun this seemingly insurmountable task with trepidation, she now felt an equally overwhelming sense of hope. Simply formulating a plan was a big moment for her.

"It's amazing how much better I feel," she said, looking over her checklist of tasks that would bring her office under control. "Now all I have to do is to move forward, one check at a time." Doreen had tamed the monster, and she knew victory was in reach.

The Career Counselor Counsels Herself

Jessica was a colorful, quirky adviser in Hawaii with a very successful business counseling displaced executives on how to get back on a successful career track. She had to acquaint herself with material from many different professions. Her "system" was to lump the information she collected into dozens of piles, like mini-volcanoes always threatening to blow.

She knew it would take a week of filing to sort through all the papers, but she had no intention of taking time from her busy schedule to actually do the deed. She had tried in the past to clear her office of the piles. It never stayed clear for long.

She worried that clients lost some of their much-needed confidence in her when they entered her disheveled digs. And her dream was to have a clear desk, where she could greet clients and be able to work efficiently in face-to-face meetings. Finally, she resolved to turn her counseling eye on herself. She took a critical look around and assessed the mess.

The paper piles weren't the only problem. She realized they were the result of a bad filing system leaking out of overstuffed cabinets. With a sigh, she started by making a quick list of all of the categories of papers and other items on her desk. Her plan was to move ahead from there, rather than try to salvage a filing system that clearly didn't work.

Using the step-by-step planning system she prescribed for clients, she listed a series of steps she committed to take. First, she determined to buy a quality filing cabinet. Then, she grouped the desktop papers into file folders according to the categories on the list she'd created. Things were becoming clearer!

Grasping the vision of what her newly organized office could mean to her image and her productivity, a determined Jessica put on her coat and headed to the nearest office supply store to order the filing cabinet and pick up more filing supplies. She was on her way!

> **FACTOID:** Information workers spend between 20 and 40 percent of their time manually searching for documents.[5]

What You Really Want

Now let's turn our attention to *your* office. But before you start getting down to business, stop a minute.

Though it's a natural tendency, don't jump into the project right away. Just because you have the opportunity (your kids are at the movies and the house is empty, or you've come to the office on a Saturday so nobody will interrupt you as you work), that's no reason to start mindlessly doing activities like labeling files, moving books off the floor, straightening piles, or rearranging stuff.

What you need first is a plan of action. If you start without a clear plan, after five hours of vigorous effort the place will look worse than when you started. The piles will just be in different places.

Instead of whirling into the job, follow the examples of Doreen and Jessica. Step back and take a moment to evaluate seriously and specifically what you really want for your office.

Slowing down to make a plan won't necessarily keep you from making rapid progress. Stopping to make a plan can actually propel you to move more quickly toward positive change.

With plan in hand, Doreen was able to quickly set about reclaiming control of her running-wild workspace. First, she toted in several boxes and commandeered help from colleagues, asking them to sort mail into manageable piles: catalogs, personal correspondence, money matters, junk mail, and mission business. That gave her a head start on handling each piece effectively and efficiently.

She also set about finding a bookcase, a filing cabinet, and a hutch for her treasures. In hours, her office was transformed. Planning was the key to her success.

In a similar way, Jessica got off to a good start after first making a plan. She made quick work of depositing her material into files in the categories she'd listed. It wasn't a perfect system (we'll show you a far better one), but it was a big improvement over the piling system that had embarrassed her and stalled her efficiency.

In the past, she'd had to hunt for papers she needed, shuffling through stacks. Now she could locate what she needed.

With the momentum she'd built up, she made more improvements, getting brighter lighting and upgrading her office chairs. A large wicker basket to hold incoming material neatly made the transformation complete.

Make a Plan!

Planning is the most important, but often overlooked, key to a successful office-organizing project. Once the enthusiasm for getting the job done has taken hold, it's difficult to delay action long enough to devise a strategy.

People who struggle to stay organized generally aren't the list-making type. For us, the motto "Just Do It" is the way to attack most projects.

Although we prefer to move forward using the seat-of-our-pants approach, this is a moment where self-control (gasp!) needs to come into play.

Resolve to make some kind of plan before moving forward, even if it's just tacking up a magazine picture of your ideal office. Techies might prefer to create an outline on the computer. Creative types might write a couplet, a poem, or a song to summarize their office hopes.

Communicate with yourself using whatever style motivates you best. Post your plan at an easy eye level. Check off the steps as they're done.

You might try formulating your vision like this: stand at the entrance to your office and look around. Pretend the office is not *your* office. Pretend you're an important client, or your boss, or your mother-in-law. Do you hear the words, "How can you work like this!" echoing in your ears?

To help you really see everything more clearly, cup your hand into a spyglass and scan the different areas of your office. Seriously. (You could also use an empty toilet paper roll for your spyglass, but we wouldn't advise it if anybody else is around.)

The results will be amazing. Clutter that long ago faded into the background will suddenly pop out with startling clarity and beg to be organized. Distancing yourself emotionally will help you evaluate the space from a more dispassionate and rational vantage point.

Moving a Step Forward

For the moment, ignore the issues that could hold you back. So you don't have the equipment you need, or the money to buy it. So your space is too small, or your boss probably won't okay any big changes.

Ignore those rational thoughts, for now. Instead, shift into dream mode, where problems can be easily resolved. Ask yourself the question Doreen asked herself: "If everything were perfect, how would it be?"

You might decide:

- "I would have a bookshelf large enough to hold all my books." Forget the fact that you don't have that piece of furniture handy, and don't have the money to buy it. Ignore the fact that you don't know where you would put a bookshelf. We're dreaming, remember! And if everything really could be perfect, you'd not only have the bookshelf but plenty of room for it and the money to buy it too.

Think as though money, time, energy, and ability are unable to throw obstacles in your path. Continue with your dreams. "If everything were perfect . . ."

- "I would have two filing cabinets, instead of one rusty little one."
- "The space wouldn't look like this. It would be neat, even beautiful."
- "I'd be able to find what I need, when I need it."
- "My boss (or co-workers or family) would stop making unpleasant comments about how things look."
- "I would use notebooks for various projects, and have them sit on the shelf for easy access, instead of filing them."

Your dreams may be very different. That's great. That means your dream pump has been primed. Now let it flow!

Wish It . . . and Reveal Clues
to the Best Solutions for *You*

Your hopes for your office provide far more than useless fantasy. Explored in detail, they reveal answers already rattling around in your head. Taking time to visualize your deeply desired office and make a wish list will likely reveal valuable clues like these:

- **"I'd have more filing cabinets."** If this is your desire, it feels like a chore to unearth filed papers. You need to make filing a lot more convenient by putting cabinets where they're within easy reach, and putting a filing system in place that really works. (That's coming soon!)
- **"It wouldn't look like this. It would be neat."** Your office probably requires some deep-down organizing and decision making. You probably need to do a significant amount of discarding and rearranging. Storage space is lacking and there's no place to put things away. Neatness is good, but not if it means that things are just thrown into drawers so they'll be hidden.
- **"I would be able to find what I need, when I need it."** A workable, reliable filing system includes a master list—a guide for filing items consistently, so they can be retrieved when needed. (More about this later.)
- **"Everyone would stop complaining about my office."** If you have a system that works for you, clearing off surfaces will work wonders to silence the chronic grouser.
- **"I would use notebooks for projects and ignore the filing cabinet,"** or **"I'd get a filing cabinet, instead of using these messy notebooks!"** You need a system that works for you and suits your personal style. If you like notebooks, use them! If you hate them, don't—use a great filing system. Read on!
- **"I would have places to put everything."** Find more space by emptying cabinets and drawers of unused items and reorganizing what you must keep. Active files and often-used items need to be within easy reach—items used less often can be tucked away in deeper storage.

Smart Steps in the Right Direction

Flip now to chapter 20, "Smart and Useful Ideas," beginning on page 207, to continue creating a powerful tool that can help you stay on track in your organizing by answering these questions:

4.1. Name something positive about your office as it is.

4.2. Write your own personal wish list of what you want for your office in great detail, perhaps using the ideas above as inspiration for your ideas. Describe everything your office would be if money, time, effort, and permission didn't play a part.

Mini-Quiz

1. Have you given serious thought to the best placement of your furniture?

2. Is every valuable space in your office well used?

3. Do you know if your office configuration is L-, U-, H-, or V-shaped?

If you answered "no" to the questions above, you'll be on the path to success when you read the next chapter.

Two-Minute Organizing Quiz

1. I feel in control of my office.

2. I immediately put things where they belong.

3. I keep a well-organized filing system.

4. My projects move forward well.

5. I keep my email in-box cleared.

6. All inappropriate, broken, and nonworking things are gone.

7. My calendar or planner works well for me.

8. The papers on my bulletin board are fresh and current.

9. My furniture looks good and works well.

10. I balance my work and family life.

Tally five points for each "yes."

50–40 points—Congratulations! You're doing really well! May we stop in and learn some of your tricks?

39–30 points—Doing good! Make a few key improvements and you'll be flying high.

29–20 points—Help is on the way. Apply the techniques in this book and you'll be a much happier camper, producing work much more efficiently.

19–1 points—Keep this book with you at all times! But seriously, it really is your lifeline to sanity and productivity. Slowly address your areas of greatest need and your office will become your best business partner. Otherwise, you are sunk!

5

Join the Office Treasure Hunt

All glory comes from daring to begin.
Eugene F. Ware

Action Highlights

By the end of this chapter, you'll be prepared to:

- Sketch a schematic of your office.
- Search for hidden spaces.
- Decide what office configuration best meets your needs, and why.

Dreaming is the fuel that powers the wonderful changes you're about to make. But you need a map to get where you want to go.

Brad's Story

Brad often worked from his fourteenth-floor condominium in Miami. Large windows in every room overlooked the deep-blue Atlantic Ocean. Thick rugs carpeted the floor of his jewel-toned living room. At sunrise, the sky awakened with wide splashes of color, and at night twinkling lights from a faraway island resort dotted the darkness.

Brad was proud of the ambiance he had created, and he loved to share it with others. Statues adorned the hallways. Large, vibrant paintings hung on the walls, and everything appeared to be in the right place. His home was a work of art.

It would have, could have, should have been wonderful, but . . . Brad had dedicated a large room as his home office. Therein was the problem.

When visitors looked from his lovely living room through an open archway into his office area, they were startled by what they saw. Clutter spilled from every surface and filled every corner. Brad was embarrassed by the mess, and he sensed that his visitors were embarrassed for him.

As a telecommuter, he didn't have to go into his corporate office very often. That was a benefit—but he paid a high price for that convenience. Office clutter had invaded his otherwise glamorous home.

His polished wood desk and ergonomically designed desk chair were buried beneath piles of papers. Brad knew he had to get it under control.

"I made the mess. I can fix it," he reassured himself. "I could just throw everything away, then start over again."

But that wasn't practical.

He thought hopefully, *Maybe it will all blow away in a hurricane.* Another not-so-great solution.

The truth was, many of the papers piled around were important and had to be saved. As Brad stepped over foot-high piles on the way to his desk, he visualized a clean office.

He began to grab papers poking out of piles, and began reading them and sorting them into categories.

"This is taking much longer than I thought," he moaned after a few hours. He knew he wanted clear surfaces, with important papers properly stored and easily found when needed. The obvious solution was to set up a functional filing system.

Being an engineer, Brad decided it made sense to draw a simple schematic of the room and sketch out a new, better arrangement of his office furniture.

He changed the position of his desk so that it faced the bay. What a pleasant view! On his schematic, he tried placing the credenza directly behind his desk, allowing for easy reach of all of his office supplies. *Now I won't need to keep them on the top of my desk*, he thought happily, *and I'll be able to keep my desktop clear!*

If things were perfect, he realized, he'd have a bigger bookshelf. So he drew one that was wider and taller. In his sketch, he relocated the fax machine from the credenza to the top of a bookshelf already positioned along a side wall.

As he scratched away with his pencil, creating his dream office, he began to see everything in the space from a new perspective. And as he studied the piles of paper, he had an "ah-ha!" moment.

Suddenly, he realized all the papers that needed to be sorted into files could never fit in the lone file drawer in his desk. So on his design, he drew a new filing cabinet—a five-drawer model with room to expand and space for office supplies.

As he drew the possibilities, he plotted out places for equipment, supplies, books, and everything else he needed to do his job. In just a few minutes, he'd taken a major step in making his dream a reality. Now he had a blueprint of what his office could be. All he needed was to implement it.

Because he was afraid his sketch would get lost amid the clutter, he taped it to the wall. "Whew," he sighed, and walked smiling into the kitchen for a cup of coffee. The hard part was over.

FACTOID: The *Boston Globe* reported that when 2,544 office workers in the

United States and Europe were surveyed, three out of four agreed with this statement: "I find myself becoming more stressed when everything is a mess and I can't find important documents when needed."[6]

X Marks the Spot: Unearthing Hidden Spaces in Your Office

When Brad reentered his office, refreshed, he saw the space in a more objective way. He noticed there wasn't room to store all the important business materials he needed because of the nonbusiness items that had oozed in from his living area over the years. When he jettisoned these, his office immediately looked more businesslike and attractive.

Like Brad, you probably have more useful empty space than you've ever imagined. Many offices, especially home offices, become dumping grounds for miscellaneous overflow. Shoes, vases, papers from another era, napkins, and plasticware take up space in drawers, nooks, cabinets, on shelves, and on the floor.

Those intruders occupy space needed for your *real* office items. Envision them gone. The space you've been lacking is revealed like buried treasure.

Another likely hidden gem of available space is the file drawer. Often, it sits relatively empty while papers that need to be filed form messy stacks on top. Imagine the papers filed neatly in the drawer in a way that allows you to quickly do the job and then find what you need later.

You want things to be neatly tucked away, but you probably don't have the space to store everything. Time to unearth more treasure and make the space you need.

To do that, you simply must evict squatters that never should have taken up residence in your office in the first place.

That pile of professional journals sitting on the floor can be stacked tidily in the closet space your extra shoes were occupying. Notes from a recent conference can go into the space now occupied by out-of-date materials from a seminar so far in the past, you'd be wise to (gasp!) discard them altogether.

Is all of the furniture in your office necessary? Most offices require basic pieces: a cabinet, or multiple cabinets, for filing; a credenza or bookcase, or both; and a computer workstation or desk.

But some unnecessary pieces may be taking up valuable space that could be used more efficiently.

Consider this: work areas that receive clients require seating. But in office spaces where workers accomplish all their tasks without visitors, chairs can go to make way for more useful pieces of furniture.

A table supporting the once-obligatory fax machine may be able to be retired too, now that its resident is rapidly becoming obsolete.

Once you start paying attention, you'll find acres of space (okay, maybe not acres . . . but a lot!) occupied by items that can be moved out. Free it up, and you can start using it right away.

Or you might just keep in mind that it's there, ready to be emptied when you need it. Mark Xs on your schematic wherever these hidden space-possibilities can be found. Your drawing is now becoming a treasure map!

Charting a Course for a Fabulous Furniture Layout

The arrangement of furniture can enhance the flow of work in your office—or slow it down. Pieces often land in specific locations because of the placement of windows, doors, and electrical outlets. But that still usually leaves several possible furniture layouts. Your task is to determine which will best meet your needs. Here are a few possible configurations.

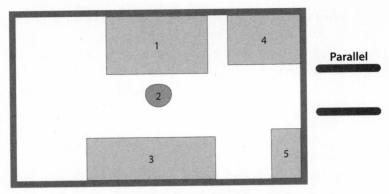

1. Desk   2. Chair   3. Credenza   4. Computer workstation
5. File cabinet   6. Bookshelves

Parallel. In this arrangement, the desk faces out with the credenza behind you. This common layout is useful when your work requires that you sit across from a client. But it doesn't allow much workspace on the desk, and you may find yourself creating piles of works-in-progress on the credenza behind you. If you can't add an additional work surface, designate an empty file drawer to hold "just for now" papers associated with current projects. That will give you a space to stow them and will keep them from piling up in an unsightly mess.

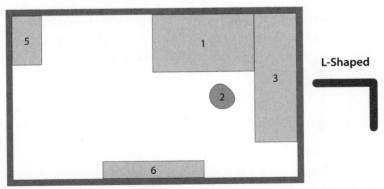

L-Shaped. In this layout, the desk surface is adjacent to a side surface, making a convenient area for a printer, fax, or other item needed within easy reach while leaving the desktop to function as a work surface. A larger work area still may be needed, though.

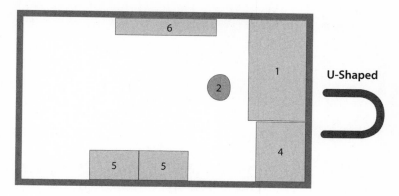

U-Shaped. Here, the desk surface is three-sided, allowing for ample workspace and room for often-used equipment to be at your fingertips.

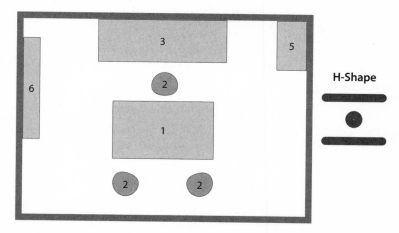

H-Shaped. This is similar to the parallel configuration, with extra shelves or cabinets for equipment and storage.

V-Shaped. Similar to the U-shaped office, this arrangement uses the desk as the corner. Like its cousin, it allows you to conveniently reach everything from your desk chair.

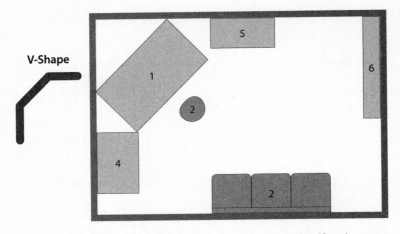

V-Shape

If you have the space, the U- and V-shaped office layouts usually are the most convenient for accessing supplies and equipment, while retaining workspace. Parallel and H-shaped offices are the best layouts for meeting with visitors. The L-shaped office is best for maximizing a small space.

FACTOID: When the National Association of Professional Organizers surveyed consumers nationwide in 2008, 27 percent said they feel disorganized at work, 91 percent said they would be more effective and efficient if their workspace were better organized, and 28 percent said having an organized workspace would save them more than an hour per day, and 27 percent said they would save at least a half hour.[7]

Smart Steps in the Right Direction

Flip now to chapter 20, "Smart and Useful Ideas," beginning on page 207, to continue creating a powerful tool that can help you stay on track in your organizing by answering these questions:

5.1. Identify things in your office that are taking up space without serving a vital purpose. List them here.

5.2. If you were to free up space, what could you move into your office to make it function better?

5.3. Which layout would work best for your office? Why? What would you have to do to implement it?

5.4. Draw a quick schematic of your office as you want it to be. Pay special attention to the placement of the large, basic pieces of furniture.

Mini-Quiz

1. Do you want a proven method for deleting clutter quickly?

2. Is your tendency to start by tackling the hot spots of disorder in your office?

3. Is your office easy to clean and beautify?

If you answered "yes" twice, and then answered "no" on question 3, you'll find relief in the next chapter.

6

Set Sail into Deeper Waters

Whatever you can do or dream you can, begin it; bold-
ness has genius, power, and magic in it.

Johann Wolfgang von Goethe

Action Highlights

By the end of this chapter, you'll be prepared to:

- Use white office storage boxes with detachable lids to
  de-clutter quickly.
- Clear surfaces, sorting papers and other items into workable categories.
- Clean and beautify your reclaimed surfaces to gain inspiration and renewed energy.

Finally! You've done the necessary background work. Now
you're ready to stop looking at the treasure map and to begin
the real digging—possibly at a surprising place.

The natural tendency is to start by attacking the mess. When you're desperate to bring order to a space, it seems reasonable to tackle cluttered hot spots first, like a jumbled bookcase or papers piled on a chair. You've patiently waited and made your plan. You want to begin. But it's still not quite time to start rearranging.

Now is the time to make the space *look* neat. Psychologically, it's much easier to work in a space that appears neat, rather than in a cluttered area where undone tasks relentlessly call your name from every direction.

Working in a cluttered room can be demoralizing. Feeling incompetent, we emotionally beat ourselves up about the mess. Those feelings are counterproductive when we're trying to accomplish a challenging task, like doing a complete organizational overhaul.

But when a space appears neat, we feel more in control. We can put aside those negative feelings while we work. The appearance of the office is no longer a constant source of pressure.

To get started, focus on this one thing—clearing surfaces. For now, forget about organizing the cluttered hot spots. Read on to see how this tip changed everything for Eileen.

Eileen Makes Magic with Seven Empty Boxes

Eileen is single and balancing a career as a special education teacher at an elementary school with a side business selling cosmetics. Her habit is to run in from work each evening, pile her school papers on a chair, and tell herself, "I'll grade those later."

Then she rushes into her home office, planning to call prospective clients to request orders and try to set up sales appointments, the key to success in her home business.

But instead she starts shuffling papers, looking for names of prospects amid brochures and order forms spread around the desk. Eventually, she throws up her hands, shaking her head in frustration as she exclaims, "Maybe I put them in the drawer, or on the credenza, or on the pile in the hallway!" She beats herself up as she sees time being wasted in unproductive efforts.

Then comes the usual internal dialogue: *I did it again! Why can't I keep the things I need in their proper places? What's the matter with me? Maybe I just don't deserve to be successful!*

It's not that she doesn't have enough time for the side business. But because she's not organized, the time she has is wasted. So she never seems to make any progress.

In desperation one evening, Eileen abandoned her paper-by-paper search method, and turned to attacking what she saw as her biggest problem—the need for a neat-looking office space.

"Maybe I'll *work* better, if my work area *looks* better," she told herself. "It sure couldn't be worse."

With determination, Eileen began gathering renegade papers from their far-flung spots in the office and placing them into white boxes she'd picked up from an office supply store for a past project.

First, she cleared the largest surface, the floor. Then she moved to the next-highest surface, the chair seats.

To help her recall which group of papers were placed in each box, she labeled them by their previous locations: under the window; from the bookshelf; under the desk; off the credenza; by the door.

One by one, she assembled the boxes and filled them, moving methodically upward from the floor to chair seats, the desktop, and the top of the filing cabinets, clearing every space. By the time she was finished, seven full boxes were stacked neatly (let's hear clapping at this point)—and all paper clutter had vanished!

One box was full of magazines, catalogs, and fliers culled from the stacks. One box labeled "Urgent" held long-misplaced, important papers she'd spotted as she worked.

She returned a pair of shoes, a lost glove, her nephew's teddy bear, her golf clubs, three coffee cups with mold growing inside, a dusty plaque, a suit jacket, and other debris that somehow sneaked into her office to their rightful homes. Removing those items made a giant leap forward in how neat the room looked.

After three hours, Eileen looked around with satisfaction at her newly cleared office. Four boxes were stacked neatly in a corner; two were tucked under her desk. Another box brimming with magazines was ready to be donated to the library at school.

Eileen was thrilled. Now she could get to work doing the tasks the office had been set up to help her do—call potential clients and make sales.

She couldn't remember a time when her office had looked so good. She quickly retrieved her call list from the box marked "Urgent" and sat down to call clients. In a short time, she'd booked three appointments. Smiling, she mused, "I should have done this years ago!"

She felt a surge of power as she realized that her business office really could become a moneymaker, not just a time-waster. Inspired, she polished surfaces that had been covered with clutter for years. She decided to buy a plant for the credenza. And she set her Roomba robot vacuum to work where it had never gone before—at least not for a very long time.

Breathing a sigh of relief, Eileen vowed, "I'll never let those piles develop again." She still had a way to go to get organized. But at least she was already reaping the benefits from tackling the first step—just clearing surfaces to make the office appear neat and tidy.

If the Shoe Box Fits . . .

Jared worked with two other people in the office of a large condominium development company. Like the three little pigs, each co-worker represented a different style of work. Jared's low-walled cubicle was between those of his two co-workers. The gal to his right kept her office bare. It was stark—really not Jared's style, at all.

To his left was a disaster area inhabited by the other man in the office. Even though Jared didn't struggle with mountains of clutter like that "little pig," he knew being neater could boost his efficiency. And he felt sure it would relieve some of the stress of trying to keep up with projects.

Because his job was to represent the company at trade shows, Jared had an abundance of hard-to-tuck-away items. Presentation materials like flip charts, an easel, candy dishes, and a pile of promotional key chains and calendars vied for space next to piles of sign-in sheets and vendor lists. Then there was the regular office stuff: mail, meeting minutes, journals, business cards, and papers that needed attention such as memos to review and proposals to edit.

Every available space in his office was occupied: the closets, the floor, every corner of the room, even his car trunk. Meetings, phone calls, and travel took time from his already harried life away from the office.

Jared's life required a high level of organization. He knew he needed to address the problem of an increasingly cluttered office or he'd end up like the guy to his left. Like Eileen, he decided to first aim just to clear his space so he could think better.

He rustled up a five-shelf bookcase. Into clear plastic shoe boxes, he deposited the little items scattered around his office: the key chains and little calendars for clients, whiteboard markers, a holder for his eyeglasses and the accompanying screwdriver, some change, and a ceramic heart from an old girlfriend.

When he could, he put like things together and labeled the boxes: "Giveaways," "Markers," "Pens," etc. When there were only one or two of a certain item, he grouped them into a box labeled "Assorted."

He put frequently used items within easy reach. He stowed seldom-used items in higher or lower places. He knew that white storage boxes with detachable lids would be ideal. When not needed, they can be taken apart, flattened, and stored for next time or simply discarded.

He placed nonurgent papers in one box, magazines and journals in another, and important papers in yet another. Promotional items went in other boxes, and he labeled each one with sticky notes.

When organizing his long-neglected desk drawers, Jared used the same principles, grouping like things together and placing the things he used often within easy reach and things used less often in the harder-to-reach spots.

A small change that made the office appear instantly less cluttered was corralling the scattered business cards into one small, clear box. "Whew!" he breathed. Having a litter-free desk instantly brightened his outlook.

Now Jared could sit back and feel good about his office. Now he could think. Now he could begin the creative work he was hired to do.

He resolved to stay twenty minutes later at work each day until he'd filed all stray papers and stored all other out-of-place items that lay waiting for him within the tidy-looking boxes.

FACTOID: According to a study of 2,544 office workers, 43 percent described themselves as disorganized, and 21 percent have missed crucial work deadlines. Almost half said disorganization causes them to work late at least two or three times each week.[8]

FACTOID: Experts with the Centers for Disease Control and Prevention say that 80 percent of our medical expenditures are stress-related.[9]

The Skinny on Desk Drawers

All desk drawers are not created equal. But every one is valuable because of its proximity to where you do your work.

The key to using these handy storage areas effectively is this: organize them using the principle of keeping similar items together. And don't let them become stagnant receptacles for unused belongings.

You can begin organizing your drawers by creating a schematic of your desk. Sketch out all your drawers, showing their locations, just as Brad drew a model of his office in chapter 5.

Next, decide on paper what kinds of items should be placed in each drawer. Think about which items are most important to have within easy reach while you work at your desk.

Consider the offices of XYZ Accounting, where all account executives had the same style desk. Each had a center drawer and three drawers on the left side. On the right side were two drawers, including one for files.

James, the analyst, used his center drawer to hold the items that used to clutter his desktop—stamps, coins, photos, notepads, extra ink, used sticky notes, and a legal pad. His drawer schematic showed the top left drawer held pens, pencils, and markers. The middle drawer on the left held "stickies," which to James meant materials that make things stick together—tape, glue, paper clips, staples, and two staplers. In the bottom left drawer he kept unused legal pads. On the right side, he kept blank forms and the files of important clients. Everything he needed was at his fingertips, and James was never without his supplies.

Keenan, the office manager, used his drawers in a much different, yet equally effective, way—because it was customized to meet *his* needs. He didn't want to fill his drawers with supplies he could easily retrieve from the central closet. So he kept "To-Do" piles in his drawers.

For Keenan, the top left drawer was where "Urgent" projects resided. The middle left drawer held his "Important-

Not-Urgent" papers, and the bottom drawer was reserved for his "I'd-better-not-lose-these" files.

He used the top center drawer for writing instruments, keys, and change. The file drawer on the right held personnel files and personal papers. The extra drawer contained a small basket of miscellaneous items he was reluctant to get rid of even though he knew he probably should, things like unidentifiable keys, coins, small promotional gifts, locks without keys, a stray button, etc.

Though James and Keenan organized their desks in completely different ways, they both kept their desk surfaces clear and stayed on top of their work, proving that as long as you have a predetermined system, you can keep your work in order and your office clutter-free. With everything neatly contained, they were able to keep track of current projects, making them easy to retrieve.

There's another trick too. Label each drawer with its purpose. A label is not only a reminder, it's a commitment. It holds you accountable to put things in their proper places right away, instead of piling them.

And be sure to use your valuable drawer space responsibly. It shouldn't become a dumping ground for junk, or a just-for-now receptacle when you're scraping off the top of your desk to tidy up for an unexpected visitor. It requires a bit of careful thought to put your drawers to work for you in a way that makes you more efficient. But once you do that, you'll be able to sail forward swiftly through the rest of your organizing makeover.

By making their spaces simply appear more tidy, and by organizing their desk drawers, Eileen, Jared, James, and Keenan stumbled onto two very important—but largely ignored—secrets of successful organizing. Tidy surfaces and organized drawers can quickly give you both the look and feel of organization.

Clutter-free work surfaces and floors empower a messy person in a way few people understand until they experience it.

What's in *Your* Desk?

As hands-on professional organizers, we have pulled some, uh . . . unusual items from clients' desk drawers, including, in one surprising case, a clean pair of underwear. These items also clearly needed relocation:

- Jumper cables (for office work?)
- Footwear
- Baby pacifier (with no baby in the office)
- Car battery
- Old, corroded batteries
- Baseball glove
- One wheel from an office cart
- Empty raisin boxes and other used food containers
- Torn-open, empty envelopes
- Expired coupons
- Ten-year-old receipts from purchases
- Twist ties
- Recipes
- Vacation postcards
- Empty cosmetics containers

Look around your office. See all that stuff that's piled on your desk and your floor? Imagine what your office would be like if you swept all of that mess into "magic" storage boxes. Nice, huh?

Now, try it! De-cluttering surfaces by temporarily hiding items in "quick-clean" boxes will inspire you to move enthusiastically forward in organizing the rest of your office. Clear surfaces clear your mind for action.

Smart Steps in the Right Direction

Flip now to chapter 20, "Smart and Useful Ideas," beginning on page 207, to continue creating a powerful tool that can help you stay on track in your organizing by answering these questions:

6.1. How many small, clear storage containers do you need to quickly group like items? How will you label the boxes? And where will they be stored? Remember, things you use often need to be within easy reach, and things that are used less frequently can go in the harder-to-reach storage spots.

6.2. Make a schematic of your desk drawers. Decide which items will go in each drawer, and commit to your plan by labeling clearly. Start sorting, and enjoy the benefits.

6.3. Which items in your desk shouldn't be there? Relocate them.

6.4. How many white boxes will you need to de-junk the furniture surfaces and the floor? If you don't know, start with two multipacks. You can return the second, if you don't open it. But this job usually takes more boxes than we originally guess.

6.5. Work on clearing one surface at a time, using your quick-clean boxes. Be sure to label them in a way that makes sense for you, such as location of the original stack.

Mini-Quiz

1. Are you using vertical surfaces to their greatest potential to relieve clutter on horizontal surfaces?

2. Are you well prepared to work on the go?

A "no" to either means you'll benefit greatly from chapter 7.

7

File Drawers and Wall Mounts and Tools, Oh My!

> Organizing your work space is the first step to turning your tiny stream of effort into a mighty river of productivity. Rewards follow.
>
> E. Roth

Action Highlights

By the end of this chapter, you'll be prepared to:

- Notice elements interrupting workflow in your office.
- Identify space-stealers and put them in their place.
- Harness the power of vertical surfaces.

Your office needs to fit you and your needs. Maybe when you set up your office, you didn't give much thought to what would really work best for you. Or maybe you inherited space left over from the person before you. Or maybe you stepped into a generic one-office-fits-all environment. Now you need to make that space really serve you, so you can be at your best on the job. How?

There's no need to traipse off to Oz and take on any wicked witches. You simply need to use the right tools. Heel-clicking is completely optional.

Erin's Deceptively Simple Solution to a Serious Problem

Since Erin started her law practice with one part-time secretary, her client list had swelled tremendously.

Friendly, compassionate Erin specialized in helping couples adopt special-needs children. Because her own child had special needs, she was passionate about seeing other children like hers placed into warm, loving families.

Unfortunately, her organizational skills had not kept up with her legal success. Her secretary managed the legal files well, but Erin's personal office looked like a paper blizzard just had blown through.

Loose papers and files she was referencing were piled on the windowsills, obstructing her view of the Manhattan skyline. Towers of paper, like a skyline of chimneys, rose from the floor. Files, memos, and legal pads were on every available surface. The floor was impassable in spots.

"It's like walking through a maze," Erin lamented. "My clients probably worry I'll lose their important documents."

And she had to admit, sometimes she actually *did* lose important documents. Erin sat among papers, ate among papers, walked among . . . you get the idea.

Her secretary couldn't keep up with the filing. After all, there were phone calls to make and other important work to be done for clients. *Maybe the filing is just not our major priority*, Erin thought, shaking her head in remorse.

Although she was a very capable attorney, she was failing at paper management. This was not comforting to clients.

Her excellent legal skills weren't something tangible they could see. But they were very aware of the mess in her office. Erin was becoming conscious that her disorganization could seriously mar her professional image.

Things changed when Sahbrah blew into the office as an intern. Sahbrah was one of those naturally organized types who never let life get out of control.

Now is my chance, thought Erin, who knew her secretary was already vastly overworked. She set Sahbrah to work on (tah-dah!) the paper blizzard.

Moments into the task, Sahbrah began building a big-picture view of Erin's problem. And, to her, the solution was simple.

As she tried to file the offending papers in the two-drawer cabinets Erin had brought from home when she set up her office, Sahbrah noticed immediately that it was almost impossible to use them. No wonder Erin had resorted to piling papers!

The cheaply made drawers were hard to pull out and only opened halfway. When they got full, they often fell off the track. Sahbrah was amazed they had even been allowed to stay in the office.

Never one to beat around the bush, Sahbrah stated the obvious plainly. "Erin, these drawers are for the birds. You need way more drawer space than this. No wonder you've got papers everywhere. I think it would help you to get a new and better filing cabinet."

Erin agreed and ordered one. And while she waited for the delivery, Sahbrah turned her attention to the office layout with an eye to creating an efficient workflow.

With her permission, and while Erin was out, Sahbrah rearranged the large pieces of furniture using the H-shaped configuration. That would give Erin space to spread work out around her desk while allowing her to sit closer to her clients when they came in for a conference.

Sahbrah also sorted papers, installed three plastic trays on the wall for files, and brought in a much bigger trash can to replace the one that had perpetually overflowed. She moved as much as she could from the cluttered surface areas to storage areas she created by mounting literature racks on the wall.

In a few days, a sturdy four-drawer filing cabinet arrived. As promised in the catalog, it had high-sided drawers that extended smoothly and fully and were equipped to keep hanging files securely locked. In hours, Sahbrah had sorted renegade papers into secure files.

Erin was thrilled. With the new office layout and better tools for managing paper, she no longer struggled to keep surfaces tidy. All it had taken to begin maintaining organization in her office was a carefully planned layout and the right tools. She was grateful for the lessons about organization she'd learned from her intern, even long after Sahbrah moved on to her own successful legal practice.

Making Your Hang-Ups Work for You

You may feel like your office surfaces are hopelessly cluttered and there's just no way to relocate all the things vying for space. Hang in there! You likely have an untapped and plentiful resource. Your walls! Used wisely, they're more valuable than any jeweled fortification in the Emerald City.

There are a plethora of gadgets for putting your biggest office space-stealers in their place—on the wall, the side of a cabinet, or the back of a door. Many of your office tools probably already have built-in mounting brackets you never noticed. Imagine the space you'd gain and the way clutter would disappear if you neatly relocated items from the desk, shelves, and cabinet tops to one of the many vertical surfaces available. Improve your office by moving some of these:

- File organizers
- Speakers
- Telephone

- Framed pictures and awards
- Light fixtures
- Pencil sharpener
- Calendar
- Magazine and catalog rack
- Clock
- Maps

 FACTOID: In a Léger Marketing survey, 90 percent of respondents who described themselves as disorganized also reported that it negatively impacted their lives. Forty-three percent said they felt stressed; 39 percent felt frustrated; 14 percent said they were upset; and 11 percent said their disorganization made them feel like a failure.[10]

A Few More Tips

Of course, as you start putting your office in order, it's important to remember a few more things. First, don't overorganize. Sometimes it's best to make do with a simple solution when a more complicated one wouldn't really be any better. For example, maybe you've realized a Rolodex or a business card notebook could keep your collected cards in order. But wouldn't an empty business card box or even just a rubber band keep your cards together just as well? Keep it simple whenever you can.

Also, try not to overbuy. A lot of clutter in offices comes from enthusiastically purchasing too much stuff: more mailing supplies than likely will be needed, excess amounts of stationery and business cards, duplicates of office supplies because there was a sale. Having things you don't really need puts pressure on your storage systems.

It pays to invest in your office. If you're using old equipment like a rickety filing cabinet or putting off buying tools such as wall-mounted file holders in an effort to save money, consider what that decision is really costing you. Discomfort? Embarrassment? Lost papers? A tarnished professional image? Furniture and tools that meet your needs can pay dividends in ways you might not expect.

However, you might not even need new office furniture. Sometimes all that's needed is to arrange what you have in a way that enhances the appearance of the office and provides greater functionality.

Take time today to think about what will really work best for you. Desk facing the door, wall, or window? Filing cabinets on this wall, or that one? These tools on the desk, or on the wall?

Putting a little thought into these choices can result in something spectacular—you'll enjoy your office and your work like never before. And it will boost your professional image. You may even find yourself clicking your heels together three times and repeating, "There's no place like my office."

Smart Steps in the Right Direction

Flip now to chapter 20, "Smart and Useful Ideas," beginning on page 207, to continue creating a powerful tool that can help you stay on track in your organizing by answering these questions:

7.1. Which pieces of furniture in your office are in poor condition and are making your job more difficult?

7.2. Which items are taking up precious space on flat work surfaces and can be moved to walls?

7.3. Which tools will you need?

Mini-Quiz

1. My desk and credenza (or bookcase) are well-organized to support my work.

2. I have boxes of papers waiting to be handled.

3. I have a designated plan for catching up with paper backups.

Answering "no" to numbers 1 and 3 and "yes" to number 2 means you need to carefully consider the next chapter.

8

Springboards to Effectiveness

Organizing Your Desk and Credenza

It is much better to keep up than to catch up.

Action Highlights

By the end of this chapter, you'll be prepared to:

- Make the most of the two big boys—the desk and the credenza.
- Employ effective habits for managing papers.
- Set up a pain-free system for avoiding filing backups.

Your desk and its overflow cousin, the credenza, are the hub of your productivity. When those two get mired in messiness, your effectiveness falters and your stress builds.

Clutter buildup on desks and credenzas has a myriad of causes. A person who manages time poorly and scrambles from one appointment to another leaves no time to return to papers and projects, and sometimes sloppily lays them about instead of filing them, creating anxiety when it's time to find them again.

At other times, clutter happens because there's just no plan for handling items that come into the office. Papers that aren't tightly managed can proliferate into a mess, quite literally overnight—or faster!

Sometimes the reason for mess on the desk is because the biggest order-bringing habit has been chronically ignored: if you get it out, put it back—quickly! Or as we have seen it stated before: stow as you go!

And sometimes, as we've already seen, many times the mess is due to having equipment that's not set up quite right for managing paper and projects.

That was Bryan's chief problem. And he was only vaguely aware of how seriously it was complicating his work.

Bryan's Story

Bryan was good at his job as a sales manager—very, very good. What's more, he loved his job of fourteen years. And he got along with his boss, except for one thing. Bryan's office was a wreck—and his boss hated that!

Periodically, Bryan's boss got so fed up with the clutter he'd scrape all the stray papers off the desk and credenza into a post office mail crate and shove it against the wall. (The nerve!)

It was a crude version of how Eileen boxed her things when she began organizing her office. But the method just caused more disorganization—and Bryan didn't know how to handle it. (You've got to question the sanity of a boss who would do this to one of his best producers, but he was a good boss in other ways, so . . .)

Bryan's cleared surfaces never lasted long. Piles quickly formed on his small desk. On the left side of his desk was the tallest and most important pile: To-Do items that required action. Some papers were labeled in folders; some weren't.

Papers—piled up to five inches thick—covered the rest of the top of the desk. Business cards filled in the remaining spaces, poking out from the stacks and tucked under the computer monitor and keyboard. His phone sat on a small pile of papers to his right.

His pitiful two-drawer filing cabinet sat under his only window. It was a bottom-of-the-line brand often found in paper-confused offices. It was the typical offender, designed to open only halfway.

Outside his office waited an empty, high-quality filing cabinet, with drawers that opened fully and bars for hanging file folders. It was purchased when Bryan began to suspect that his present filing cabinet was not doing the job, but he'd not made time to make the switch.

Stacking trays on the filing cabinet held a potpourri of items: empty file folders; business card holders (sans cards); and important phone numbers written on sticky notes, napkins, and scraps of paper.

Half of the very limited space on the top of his credenza held overflow from the desk. The other half held urgent, important, "can't-be-lost" papers. The problem was that sometimes the division between the two groups became seriously blurred.

But a still bigger problem loomed: the mail crates against the wall filled by his boss held a backlog of assorted papers, ranging from trash to urgent.

It is amazing Bryan worked as well as he did in this discouraging and disorderly setting.

Light Begins to Dawn

One day, Bryan happened across an article about the infamous Collyer brothers of New York City, who hoarded so much junk in their home that one brother was crushed by it while crawling through a tunnel of old newspapers with food. The other brother, who was too ill to crawl out of the mess, died of starvation in his own home.

Psychologists were still studying the sixty-year-old case with interest. Though no one knew why the Collyer brothers lived in such chaos, one thing seemed clear: they didn't make rational decisions. Bryan saw a little of that tendency in himself. He vowed to resist the clutter and reclaim his space.

I've got to make some sense of this chaos, he thought as he began working on his mess. And sure enough, as he handled one piece at a time, items seemed to fall naturally into groups. He neatly lined the grouped stacks across the top of his credenza.

Working from there, he loaded these papers into hanging file folders and stored them by category in the new filing cabinet he dragged in from the hall. He was able to work quickly because he wasn't sentimental about holding on to each paper, or perfectionist in decision making about where to put them.

When the filing cabinet became crowded, he bought another two-drawer cabinet to catch the overflow. He wisely surmised that nothing discourages the use of a good filing system like having to wrestle papers in and out of jammed-together file folders. (A good rule to follow: it's too crowded when you can't fit a fist into the remaining space.)

He saved his To-Do pile on the left for last. After sorting it into files, he stored them in the most accessible place in his office—the file drawer in his desk.

Unaware that offices are often where healthy plants go to die, he proudly placed a new plant on the cabinet under the window. He would take it home later. But for now, it was a statement of victory. It represented his new attitude on keeping his office orderly and pleasant.

For now, he resolved to focus on the high-priority items now organized in files in his desk drawer and ignore the mail crates of less important items until later.

His new mantra was, "Keep the main thing, the main thing."

On a Roll

A smart guy like Bryan could see that it would be better to keep his desktop free to use as a work surface, not as a substitute for a filing cabinet.

So he made a rule to keep from sliding into disorder again: whenever he left his desk, he'd slip the papers he was using on his current project into a designated place in the file drawer.

Many people would have just left them out and closed the office door. But Bryan realized he had to be extra careful to keep his surfaces clear, lest he begin to slip back into clutterdom.

Next, he turned his attention to the credenza. The top had held reference books and a boxful of cards he'd gathered during networking events. The cards were from clients and prospects, and some had no use to him at all. He determined to sort them into categories later.

But first, he ejected debris from inside his credenza to make room for phone books, catalogs, journals, and other bulky items. Next he cleared his desk drawers, throwing away old gum wrappers, deteriorated rubber bands, useless pens, and more.

He stowed writing instruments and keys in small containers in a drawer on the right side of his desk. In the top drawer on the left side, he placed tape, stapler, staples, glue, and paper clips. In the drawer under that, he deposited stationery and envelopes. He reserved the bottom drawer for his personal stash of snacks.

By coming in a little early and committing the first twenty minutes of each workday to the task, slowly but surely Bryan dug through and filed the papers his boss had so unceremoniously raked into mail crates. From time to time, he would snag a free salesperson to work with him on the project. After a while, the mail crates were a thing of the past and the filing cabinets were doing their job well.

In the next chapter, you'll learn how to group your To-Do files and other files so they'll become tools for smooth-running efficiency.

 FACTOID: Neatness is often listed as a criterion for judging the quality of an employee's work on standard job performance evaluations. Could organizing your office lead to a better score? And perhaps, financial reward?

Smart Steps in the Right Direction

Flip now to chapter 20, "Smart and Useful Ideas," beginning on page 207, to continue creating a powerful tool that can help you stay on track in your organizing by answering these questions:

8.1. Because they're your springboard into action, the desk, credenza, and tops of filing cabinets require special attention. Are yours chronically in disarray? Briefly, write your plan for solving that problem.

8.2. Do you need more filing cabinets, or just better ones? Do you need more space of any kind?

8.3. Have you designated a spot to hold current projects when you're not working on them? Will you commit to putting them there whenever you leave your desk?

8.4. Can you devote twenty minutes each morning to working on the backlog of papers that need proper filing?

Mini-Quiz

1. Do you rigorously follow a consistent plan for incoming papers?

2. Do you have the supplies you need to organize your papers?

3. Do you have a setup for handling random papers that might otherwise end up in a pile awaiting decisions?

Any "no" answers make the next chapter a lifeboat for you.

9

Drowning in Incoming Paper?

Here's a Lifeline

The solution will not come in a day, but it must come daily.

Action Highlights

By the end of this chapter, you'll be prepared to:

- Devise a plan to effectively manage how papers enter your office.
- Set up a system for dealing with the day's new arrivals.
- Set up a To-Do Action File for papers requiring action.

Those who struggle with papers see them as one big muddle of confusion. When we realize that the vast majority of papers—and the problems that follow them—fall into three categories, the fog begins to clear.

The Problem with Papers

Incoming Papers. Often, we fail to make a decision about a paper when it comes into the office and, instead, lay it aside somewhere "just for now." Papers leak in from all over—the mail, the briefcase, after a conference or meeting, from the hands of co-workers handing off reports, and more. They quickly pile up, awaiting attention in random areas instead of in one designated place.

Resident Papers. Commonly, there's no system for handling these over the long-term. Some require action and can't be filed until the action is complete. Some need input from someone else before they can be finalized. Some fall into the "maybe" category—people I might want to hire, places I might want to go, things I might want to do. Some need to be retained in a logical way so they can be retrieved later. Some are part of long-range projects in progress. Some are need-right-now notes. Some are part of daily business activities. And some are trash.

Action Papers. Often, a method hasn't been set up to handle papers that need immediate action—the stack of phone messages needing responses, the report handed to you when you walk in the door, or the stack of notes left for you on your chair. You need to give all of them attention quickly, but there's no consistent way to prioritize them and keep them organized. Actions are random, and your work shows it.

An office without systems in place for these three categories of paper will be a disaster, indeed. But there's good news: you're about to learn how to solve these problems in an easy, step-by-step way.

The Doctor's Rx for Incoming-Paperitis

Dr. Margarita felt like her whole life was hurry, hurry, hurry. She dropped off the kids at school and rushed into her family medical practice. As soon as she entered the office, an employee grabbed her coat and purse. Somebody else handed her the waiting stack of charts for patients already sitting in rooms.

Before she'd taken two more steps, the receptionist handed her a fistful of telephone messages. Two steps more, and a nurse usually stopped her about an emergency. Two steps later, and a pharmaceutical representative often ambushed her with a brochure, a gift, or a box of samples. By the time she made it to her piled-high desk, she slumped in a daze into her chair, with arms still full of items she'd collected since walking through the door. As another employee shoved a cup of coffee into her free hand, she resolved to tackle the day.

In the first few minutes, she'd handled the emergency, glanced at the phone messages, perused the charts of waiting patients, and rushed forward. Without fully realizing it, the doctor had set up a system—albeit a frenetic one—of handling papers on the run. Her whole life was on the run.

This wasn't what she'd envisioned when she set up her practice. And now her personal life was suffering as a result of the chaos at her office. She often didn't have time to go to soccer meetings, practices, and games. When she finally left the office each day, she was exhausted. Her work was taking over her life.

"Things have got to change!" she vowed. At the next staff meeting, she announced she was going to make changes. She listed the things that were the most troublesome, beginning with the bombardment of papers and problems she faced every morning as she walked in. The frenetic system in the office was hard on everyone who worked there. Smoothing out the rough spots could make things easier on everyone.

She described her desire for a system of handling information at the beginning of the day. Instead of having papers shoved into her hands when she walked in the door, the doctor wanted a calmer, saner way of getting information. She created a protocol for how employees should approach her in the morning.

Starting immediately, the receptionist would ask pharmaceutical reps to sign in and wait to be admitted. They would be called in as soon as Dr. Margarita could give them attention. No more popping in front of her uninvited as she passed them in the hall or waiting room.

Once she was in her office, one person was appointed to bring her the charts, messages, and emergencies to review, while someone else brought coffee. This gave her a moment to get a handle on the day before tackling any urgent matters.

The first day of the new system, Dr. Margarita could hardly believe the change. "So much calmer!" she breathed, as she strode to her office.

With a less-harried start to the day, she suddenly was able to see other problems she'd never really noticed. *I'll bet there's a better way to handle these piles of papers*, she thought, as she looked at the disheveled administration area. *And we could put together systems that reduce the amount of time patients wait too!*

She pulled out a sheet of paper and began jotting down ideas. She decided to change her office hours slightly, pushing back the first scheduled appointment of the day by fifteen minutes. That would give her fifteen minutes each morning to get organized and check in with her assistant before seeing patients. The weight of the guilt she felt when those first patients of the day were kept waiting rose from her shoulders.

To stem the flow of the river of medical brochures that rushed into the doctor's office each week, her assistant collected them in a small filing cabinet. That way, the doctor could review them when she had time, and they'd no longer form nagging piles on her desk.

Dr. Margarita also scheduled time each day to sit with her assistant to handle the patient folders and the day's mail. Things that she wanted to take home were put into her briefcase in a manila folder marked with the day's date.

When she brought them back, each document held sticky notes with instructions on what to do with each one. Every day, her assistant reviewed the folders and carried out the doctor's orders. This helped everyone. Patient charts were being updated in a more timely manner, and the staff had a new system for keeping up.

Patients noticed and complimented the doctor on the new feel in her office. Smiling, she instructed her staff to order some green plants to place in every patient room, and a large plant for the waiting room. This was the beginning of a new way to treat her patients, her staff, and herself!

Ray's Paper Chimneys

Ray had a similar problem in a different setting. His living room is his office. He's a writer, a one-man show for his magazine. He writes it, produces it, sells ads for it, and mails it out.

"Writing is power" is his mantra. And to hear him tell it, he's a very powerful man.

Various organizations are interested in his research on computer software and contact him regularly. They know he has a large distribution list, and if he writes a positive review they'll get many new customers.

Companies he features in his magazine frequently send him their latest software, ads, fliers, magazines, and computerized gadgets. And with clever self-promotion, he's earned a spot on many mailing lists. He's proud that his writing earns him many freebies, and he happily takes in baskets of promotional materials and samples. But the clutter was out of control long ago.

He needs a well-run mailroom and staff to handle his prodigious supply of daily mail. But it's just Ray. And being the creative type, he doesn't do mail well.

That's where the paper chimneys come in. Because Ray receives more mail than his mailbox can hold, his mail carrier opens the door each day and brings in the newest arrivals. Ray points to a spot on the floor, and the carrier dumps it there.

Ray flips through the stack and pulls things of interest: bills, payments, sample packages of free software, and anything handwritten. The rest stays in its stack, piled high like a chimney rising out of the floor. His floor has become a skyline, with thirty or forty stacks of varying heights, some up to two feet high.

It's difficult to navigate a path through the piles. The hallway, dining room table, and kitchen counter overflow with piles too. And most of the papers are so old they are now irrelevant.

Ray's extreme example teaches us one simple lesson about resident papers: if you don't handle them, they'll never go away. Motivational speaker Barbara Hemphill once said, "Clutter is simply postponed decisions." And the more backlog Ray created, the more he avoided making decisions about how to handle the papers that needed his attention.

A Proper Paper-Handling System

Avoiding Ray's dilemma is simple. The trick is this: handle paper as soon as it hits your desk, or at least by the end of the day. It's the only way to stay ahead. More will arrive tomorrow. And the day after that too.

Some folks like to prescribe the OHIO (Only Handle It Once) method for handling paper. That sounds good, but often it's just not practical. You may not immediately know what you want to do with that paper. For instance, you want to pay a bill that's come in, but you need to double-check the credit card statement. You want to answer a letter, but you don't have time at that moment. Sometimes you just need a mental cushion, some time to ruminate about what decision you want to make on the information found on the paper in your hands.

A more practical motto is this: each time you touch it, move paper forward into the next organizational step. That assumes you have a sensible system in place for how you store papers until you get back to them.

Don't succumb to the temptation of looking through incoming papers until you're ready to concentrate and follow through on your decision for each paper. If you look at them and then put them down, you'll have the feeling when you return to them that you've already handled them, even though you took no action the first time you saw them.

It's important to make a note about the next step—either on the paper or on a sticky note—before you put down the document. That will keep you from having to read it again when you're ready to take action.

Another nugget: designate a time to handle waiting papers. You don't want them to pile up into chimneys, right? Instead of OHIO, your method should be DAIO (Decide About It Once).

Brilliant Bob Sells Cereal Box Sides— But Can He Get Organized?

Bob's unusual advertising office was plagued with paper proliferation. Filing reference papers wasn't the problem: Bob's secretary took care of that. A bookkeeper managed all papers pertaining to company finances, so those weren't a problem for Bob either.

The papers he needed to manage related to running his wildly successful company that sold, of all things, advertising space on the sides of cereal boxes. Often Bob was so in-demand he held a phone to each ear and juggled two conversations at once. He dashed in and out of meetings and appointments all day long. His office buzzed with excitement and movement.

But Bob had no system for handling incoming papers that required his action. So they were piled everywhere.

At times, Bob would work at another desk because the clutter in his office was so distracting. But he always made a joke about it. When it became overwhelming, he'd chuckle for all to hear: "I told the supplier that I designed a new and better ad for him, but the truth is, the old one just disappeared. It dug its own grave in one of the piles."

"I have no choice but to be brilliant because I have to keep reinventing lost things," he added with a grin. But jokes aside, his situation was, in his opinion, unique, overwhelming, and insurmountable.

He believed nothing could help his problem. It bothered him terribly that he couldn't get a handle on his papers.

However, he didn't want to take time to address the problems. He simply believed that the clutter and disorganization were evils that naturally accompanied his success.

Undeterred by his skepticism, his receptionist, who'd just returned from a seminar on organizing, went to work on his desk. She set up a grouping of red, green, and yellow hanging file folders. Then she sorted the papers on his desk by topic and transferred them to the file folders, labeling them with the action that needed to be done, such as: "Pay This Bill," "Present to ABC," "Sketch for XYZ."

The red folders were labeled with tasks that were urgent: "Return to Doug Smyth at Sodas-R-Us," "Design for Robo-Pup," "Decide on/Respond Immediately." All were important assignments that easily might have been lost in his piles and forgotten.

The green folders were labeled with tasks that needed to be done, but weren't urgent: "Design New Letterhead," "Create New Job Descriptions for Staff."

Yellow folders held tasks that could be delegated, such as: "Mail Samples to Smith," "Call Johnson to Say Designs Ready for Review."

Bob's receptionist found his papers were easy to prioritize by color. In about thirty minutes, she cleared his desk, corralling all papers into appropriate folders. From then on, each incoming paper found a place in one of the groups.

Bob was surprised and delighted at the result. He still had piles around the room, but he finally had a grip on what needed to be done to handle them too. Just having a plan and feeling more in control reduced his stress—and boosted his productivity even more!

Bob followed the receptionist's lead and pitched in to help clear the piles around the room. For the next two days they worked diligently, sorting the papers into folders. Because they'd been piled for so long, many were no longer relevant and were easily discarded. At the end of the task, what remained were six open-top crates holding hanging files of red, green, and yellow.

Bob rightly reasoned that by tackling even just a handful of overdue items each day he'd clear the backlog in a few weeks. He liked the math of how that worked out. And as he unearthed papers requiring immediate action, he tackled those right away.

With less stress, the office environment improved. Bob still joked, but it didn't have the sting of disappointment. Now he joked about things that were really funny, not his lack of organization.

Sure, things would go wrong and sometimes items turned up missing, but it happened less and less as Bob's papers got more and more in control.

Even just a simple plan—such as using three colors—can quickly bring order to an otherwise chaotic office. The key is to make the plan. Then work it. Consistently. You'll no longer feel like you're drowning in the flow of incoming papers.

Smart Steps in the Right Direction

Flip now to chapter 20, "Smart and Useful Ideas," beginning on page 207, to continue creating a powerful tool that can help you stay on track in your organizing by answering these questions:

9.1. Which of the three types of papers cause the most problems in your office?

9.2. What changes could you make to build some organization time into your day?

9.3. Collect papers that require immediate attention in a container marked "Urgent."

Mini-Quiz

1. Do you have papers in boxes or piles that need to be handled in some way?

2. Do you have a plan to deal with them?

3. Are you ready to tackle the problem?

If you have a need, but no plan to solve your problem, this is the chapter for you. If you answered that you're ready to tackle the problem, let's get going by following the system in the next chapter. Don't worry. You can do it! You might even love it.

10

Getting Down to (Bigger) Business

Every worthwhile accomplishment has a price tag attached to it. The question is always whether you are willing to pay the price to attain it—in hard work, sacrifice, patience, faith, and endurance.

John C. Maxwell

The three great essentials to achieve anything worthwhile are: first, hard work; second, stick-to-itiveness; third, common sense.

Thomas Edison

Action Highlights

By the end of this chapter, you'll be prepared to:

- Divide existing papers into five critical categories.
- Devise a customized To-Do Action File to keep you on track.

Perhaps you remember Eileen, the teacher and cosmetics businesswoman from chapter 6, who cleared her office in record time. Her papers no longer cluttered her office because they had been grouped by where they had been located in her office into seven white storage boxes. Junk had been evicted from the office, old magazines had been culled and placed in a box, and urgent papers had been rescued and placed in a special box. That system was better than looking through piles scattered all over the office, but it was far from efficient. It was just the first step in getting her papers under control. Her story continues . . .

Eileen Takes Another Step

After sorting the clutter in her home office into file storage boxes, Eileen was quite pleased with the new sense of order in her life.

Then Jeri, Eileen's sponsor in her cosmetics business, dropped by. And though she was impressed by the neatness of Eileen's usually messy office, she was appalled to learn that Eileen was trying to carry on her business by dipping into the things stored in her "magic" quick-clean boxes.

"You can't run a business, or your life, out of boxes!" Jeri exclaimed.

Never shy and something of a self-styled expert in paper management, Jeri adopted an energetic, can-do attitude and was determined to help Eileen take her level of organization to the next logical step.

"Let's do this thing right!" Jeri commanded cheerfully. "Get me five empty white boxes and write what I tell you on them. I learned this method a long time ago, and I teach it to a lot of the girls in my group."

Dutifully and gratefully, Eileen assembled the boxes and printed on them as Jeri dictated:

- "To-Do" would hold files with items requiring action.
- "To File" would hold reference items that should be stored.

- "For Others" would hold things she would deliver to their new or rightful owners.
- "Pending" would hold dated items.
- "Financial" would hold bills and other financial papers.

Jeri and Eileen took the first box of miscellaneous papers that had been scooped and dumped. Quickly, they sorted them into the five new boxes.

As they worked, they discarded outdated and useless materials. They decided to leave the "Urgent" box Eileen had created and the magazine box for another day.

Working together was fun. It only took a couple of hours to sort all of Eileen's papers, and when the task was done, it was much easier for Eileen to find papers she needed because they were filed in categories. She felt control slowly moving into her office.

Eileen's To-Do Action File

"Listen, I've got to scoot pretty soon," Jeri said, when the last box was finished. "But before I go, let me get you started on a really important part of this system—it's the To-Do Action File.

"Go get those papers out of the box labeled To-Do. You have a bunch of unused hanging file folders and small plastic tabs for labeling—get those too.

"Now, deposit each individual paper or group of papers from the To-Do box into its own individual file folder. Label each file folder with a verb telling what needs to be done with each paper, such as 'Place Order' or 'Gather Materials for Appointment.'"

And so they began. Since Eileen enjoyed a neat look, she used plastic label tabs (not the upside-down sticky notes preferred by some) staggered evenly across the group of folders so they could be read easily. Each folder contained just the item or items that related to one action.

In one folder, she put a telephone bill with charges she wanted to question. She labeled the folder "Call Sprint." She put a letter from her aunt in another folder and labeled it "Answer Aunt Georgia's Letter." In another folder, she put a receipt and labeled the folder "Return Quilt." In another folder, she dropped an article she'd torn from a magazine and labeled it "Mail to Laura."

This required a lot of folders, and each one she labeled and filed gave her an increasing sense of control. Now she knew what she had to do and where she could find the associated paper.

Before she left, Jeri suggested grouping the folders using a method popularized by bestselling author and speaker Stephen Covey. She and Eileen placed dividers between the groups of folders, creating four main categories: "Urgent and Important," "Important, but Not Urgent," "Urgent, but Not Important," and "Not Important and Not Urgent."

Jeri hopped up, gave Eileen a quick hug, and left her to finish emptying the box with all of the To-Do papers inside. Filing and labeling one file folder at a time with a verb, Eileen soon had a road map prioritizing all the things she had to do. She put the open-top box holding the hanging files on her credenza, where she could easily access it. And she pledged to check it for assignments every day.

Anatomy of a Terrific To-Do Action File

As Jeri reminded Eileen, let us remind you to strongly resist the urge to group more than one thing in one folder, even if they seem similar. This way every item is listed, as if it's on a To-Do list, and nothing gets overlooked.

So be sure you have a separate folder for each person you need to call and for each particular thing you need to do. And don't worry if you use up a lot of hanging file folders or tabs. When you first get started that's perfectly normal, because you're probably behind in a lot of actions you need to handle. When you catch up by doing one action at a time and removing that folder as it is completed, your To-Do file will shrink. New items will be added and handled as needed. Here's how to get started:

- **Label each tab** beginning with a verb indicating the action to be taken. Psychologically this will motivate you to follow that implied command. And because the information is all right there, it's convenient to follow through. Hint: If you don't have detachable tabs for labeling, use upside-down sticky notes instead.
- **Corral files** in a suitable container. If you only have a few files, a small desktop file holder will work. If you have more files than will fit in a desktop file holder, it would be best to keep them in a file drawer or open-top crate. Hint: Most hanging files will fit nicely over the top edges of a plain, white storage box.
- **Group files** in a way that makes sense for you. If they're in no particular order, that's okay. (Sure beats piling!) Some people find success using the red-yellow-green groupings Bob employed. Others, like Eileen, choose Covey's groupings based on urgency and importance.
- **Select a location** for this filing system, as close as possible to where you spend the most time.
- **Thumb through** the files daily. Take care of urgent and important items first, but don't let the important-but-not-urgent items gather dust for too long.

More Relief for Eileen

By sorting the original boxes into groupings and creating a To-Do Action File, Eileen took a giant step into the world of order. The next time Jeri dropped in, she saw a working To-Do file and an active worker getting jobs done systematically.

Eileen had also tackled much of her remaining four boxes effectively.

First, she'd emptied the box labeled "For Others." She'd returned some items to their owners, then donated or recycled the rest. She vowed to no longer be a "keeper" for others.

"Pending" items—things she wanted to do that were tied to a date—were transferred to hanging folders in their own box. It held papers dealing with things to be done at some specific time in the future: concert tickets, party invitations, printouts of airline e-tickets, and fliers she needed to keep about upcoming school functions.

When she noted the date of an event on her calendar, she also added the word "Pending" as a reminder there was something in a "Pending" folder that would give her more information. That helped her avoid the panic that had always set in as she reached to find things she needed before leaving the house.

Eileen had put her bills to be paid into a holder on her desk. Bills she'd already paid went into an accordion folder that was divided by month.

Other "Financial" papers, such as insurance policies and credit card statements, went into the filing cabinet in labeled folders.

Eileen was stymied when she looked at her biggest box, the "To File" box. But Jeri promised to return soon to teach her a file-by-color system. We'll share it with you in chapter 11.

Organize for Your Family's Sake:
If Mama Ain't Happy . . .

Yvonne, a homeschooling mom of three and a work-from-home magazine editor, did a pretty good job of keeping a lot of balls in the air. Her job allowed her to set her own hours, so she worked whenever her husband could take over the homeschool lessons left for the day. But she was always on the lookout for techniques that could help her get more done in less time and give her a chance to relax with her family and sneak in some daily exercise.

It was getting harder and harder to do either of those things as her responsibilities grew and her home-office space shrank. She was becoming desperate to find ways to be better organized because she knew doing so would ease the pressure she always felt—and that would make her not only a better editor, but a better wife and mommy too.

After her third child was born, Yvonne's tidy home office was turned into a bedroom and her office moved into the living room, across from the dining room, with the home's entryway in between. That's when chaos ensued.

She didn't like the idea of having office furniture where her family greeted and entertained guests. So she donated her old metal filing cabinet to charity and transferred all her files to plastic totes tucked in her bedroom's walk-in closet.

She bought a desk with a hutch on top to put in her new office space, but it only had one shallow drawer, two glass-front cabinets, two narrow shelves, a handful of fist-size cubbies, and two small cabinet spaces. Bottom line: there was no room for files. Paper management became a constant struggle. And the growing stack of papers on her otherwise neat desk nagged her. She did her best to keep papers requiring action in view. But recently, there were so many it was becoming more and more difficult to keep important tasks from being ignored.

Meanwhile, papers she wanted to save for reference were taking over a nearby coat closet. Whenever she could, she whisked them onto one of the shelves she'd installed when she claimed the living room as her new office. But now, the piles in the closet were unmanageable. She no longer had any idea where to find anything. And she worried that important papers might become irretrievable in the clutter. She knew it made her edgy a lot of the time. "The old saying is so true," she sighed. "If Mama ain't happy, nobody's happy."

Yvonne knew she had a strong tendency to tackle all jobs with a perfectionist attitude. Having things in disarray made her uncomfortable. And when she was under extreme work pressure, untidy areas of the home made her feel almost frantic.

But she didn't know how to fix the stash of papers on her desk and shape them into workable priorities. Every time she got them under control, more slipped in and took over again. Her desk didn't look especially cluttered, but things were starting to slip through the cracks as other responsibilities mounted and the pressure increased. Recently, she'd even paid a credit card bill late—incurring a $40 fee and a black mark on her otherwise-perfect payment record.

One morning, before the rest of her family awakened, she decided enough was enough. She researched organizing techniques on the Messies Anonymous website and came up with a plan. A naturally early riser, she decided to tackle the project right away, while she still had the energy and some uninterrupted time to work.

Later, she fired off this exuberant email to Sandra, the founder of Messies Anonymous:

In my first hour of the day today, I created my To-Do Action File. I followed all the instructions, including using verbs to name the files, dividing them into the four quadrants, and color-coding the system. Wow! What a relief it is to have that sitting there obediently now, ready to serve me, in the space where my dog-eared stack used to taunt and worry me.

You can't imagine the relief just getting that stack organized into the four quadrants has brought me. Now, I'm not shuffling the Urgent and Important with the Not Urgent Not Important anymore. They all have their proper space, and I know this is a system I can continue with ease. How simple! How empowering!

The best part for me isn't that I feel more in control of my responsibilities, it's that I know how this will benefit my family. When Mama ain't happy, nobody's happy. And that old saying, sadly, has proven true in our house. When feeling out-of-control pushes me to stress overload, I am not the wife and mommy I ask Jesus to help me be every day.

It's amazing how just tackling a job that's been nagging you, but you didn't know how to accomplish, can make it feel like a bright, new day. I'm going to tackle the papers in my overstuffed closet next, using the white-box approach. I can't wait to send you the before-and-after pictures. Thank you for all you do!

Smart Steps in the Right Direction

Flip now to chapter 20, "Smart and Useful Ideas," beginning on page 207, to continue creating a powerful tool that can help you stay on track in your organizing by answering these questions:

10.1. If you've scooped all of your business papers into boxes, as Eileen did earlier, it's time to group them into the five categories: "To-Do," "For Others," "Pending," "Financial," and "To File."

10.2. After you finish the To-Do Action File, handle the items in "For Others," and arrange the files in the "Pending" and "Financial" boxes in a way that makes sense for you.

10.3. Set aside the "To File" box for now, until Jeri returns in the next chapter to explain exactly how it's done.

Mini-Quiz

1. I have a great filing system that I use easily.

2. I have a good filing system that works pretty well.

3. I need a filing system that works.

If you answered "yes" to number 1, you might want to skip the next chapter. If you answered "yes" to number 2, scan the chapter for tips. If you answered "yes" to number 3, commit the next chapter to memory and work it in detail.

11

Eat the Filing Elephant in Only Six Bites

Vital papers will demonstrate their vitality by spontaneously moving from where you left them to where you can't find them.

Unknown

Action Highlights

By the end of this chapter, you'll be prepared to:

- Create hanging files with color-coded labels.
- Alphabetize the files in each group.
- Prepare a master list of files in your system.
- Note each addition on the master list as you add folders.
- Purge unnecessary documents on a regular basis.
- Maintain your new filing system.
- Decide which papers to keep and which to toss.

Eileen Tackles the "To File" Box

As she'd promised, spunky Jeri returned to help Eileen get better organized for efficiency. The lesson of the day: filing!

"This system works like a charm because it's so simple," Jeri explained. "There are just three things you can do with a piece of paper. You can file it for future reference. You can act on it. Or you can throw it away. Get me one of those boxes and I'll show you how it works."

Before she did anything else, Jeri pulled out a sheet of paper, turned it sideways, and divided it into five columns. Holding up the paper, she announced that it was the all-important Master File List for the reference—or storage—section of Eileen's new filing system.

They'd already created a To-Do Action File in an open-top box and Eileen had been using it successfully, getting far more accomplished than ever before. But this part of the system would be arranged in a filing cabinet. Instead of labeling files with a verb, as she was doing with her Action folders, Eileen would label each of these folders with a noun, describing the person, place, or thing associated with the information it held.

The five columns on the sheet of paper would serve as a kind of key to the filing system, showing what files it held and where they'd be found.

Jeri labeled the first column "People." In that column, they'd list all the folders created to hold information about Eileen and the people in her life, including friends, family, and even pets (because they're family members too, right?).

Files in that section would include school records, medical records, and important papers like birth certificates and passports.

The second column was labeled "Places and Things." These files would hold warranties, instruction manuals, computer information, and home files. The "Places" category included directions to various locations, restaurant menus, and maps for cities visited.

In the top of the third column, she wrote "Ideas and Interests" for folders concerning information on hobbies, possible trips, recipes, and more.

The fourth column was labeled "Finances" for papers related to insurance, banking, stocks and bonds, credit cards, old tax records, etc.

The fifth column was labeled "Work." That section, Jeri explained, could hold files related to anything a person considers to be their work: school, job, a church ministry, volunteer work, and in Eileen's case, her cosmetics business.

Larger businesses would need a more complex system. But these categories fit Eileen's needs perfectly, in a format that would allow her to find what she needed when she needed it.

Before they got out the boxes holding all of Eileen's papers, Jeri explained how the Master File List system was going to work.

"It's simple," she said. "Your papers will go into the groups at the tops of the columns. As you add a file to each category, list its name in the column where it belongs. Don't worry about the order."

For the first time, Eileen glimpsed order emerging from the chaos. The master list would tell her where everything was filed. She felt relieved, even elated.

Filing will be a breeze, she thought as she picked up another paper and dropped it into a folder. *Hooray!*

Color Me Organized

Jeri helped Eileen choose different label colors to name each of the five filing sections. They selected three-inch plastic tabs, instead of smaller ones, so she'd have plenty of room to write the section names.

Eileen labeled the hanging files in the "People" section with blue. She used red labels for "Places and Things," and yellow for "Ideas and Interests." Green labels made the money-related "Finances" files easy to spot, and she used white for "Work" files.

Following Jeri's advice, Eileen chose dark green hanging files to hold her papers. Jeri said they reminded her of the ground, and the colorful tabs were the flowers. She encouraged Eileen to use manila folders only when she needed to subdivide papers contained in a hanging file folder.

Jeri then instructed Eileen to put all of the tabs on either the far right or far left side of the hanging files, alternating sides with each color section. She was not to put any tabs in the center slots. The center position would be reserved for another step that would come later, Jeri promised. "Just line them up along the sides, like soldiers standing in rows," she said.

Armed with such a smart plan, Eileen smiled and started sorting. She and Jeri opened the boxes of unfiled papers, and Eileen lifted out the top paper: an unpaid water bill. She immediately tucked that into the new bill holder she'd set up on her desk.

Next, she picked up a receipt from last week's trip to the office supply store. She tucked that into the twelve-pocket accordion file she'd set up to hold each month's receipts. Next, she found her active client list. She pulled out a white label and labeled it "Client List," then put the label in a plastic tab and attached it to the far left side of a hanging folder in the section in the file box set aside for "Work" files. Then she wrote "Client List" in the "Work" column on the Master File List.

"This makes so much sense!" Eileen exclaimed. "I should be able to get through all these papers far faster than I ever dreamed! And then I'll be able to find anything I need—in a flash!"

She continued, putting a car insurance policy update in a folder with a green label in the "Finances" section. She logged "Car Insurance" in that column on her Master File List.

She put a recent report from her doctor in a folder labeled with a blue tab, and tucked it in the "People" section, then logged it in that column.

Jeri suggested creating a memento file in the "People" section. A humor file and an inspiration file, both filled with nuggets Eileen had saved from magazines and emails, could go in the "Ideas and Interests" section. They were good for mental health, Jeri said. "That would be a good place to keep a file with favorite Bible verses, religious study materials, or other spiritual materials," she added.

Making one decision at a time, Eileen and Jeri tackled the first box. They set a timer and worked in fifteen-minute increments.

Whenever Eileen couldn't decide what to do with a particular paper, she slipped it to the bottom of the pile, to be handled at the end of the task. Jeri had explained that sometimes it's easier to know how to label something when the pile is smaller and not so overwhelming.

As Eileen worked, she alphabetized the files in each of the five sections. She didn't worry that the growing Master File List wasn't alphabetical. It was good enough just to be able to scan the names of the files in each section.

A rhythm to the job developed, and Eileen found it took about an hour to empty each box of the papers it held. As she emptied each box, she flattened it and put it aside with the other white boxes. The room was looking good! And she was feeling good because she was in control.

Eileen Finishes the Job

Finally, Eileen had emptied the "To File" boxes of their papers. Now, their contents were neatly stored in hanging files with color-coded tabs down the left and right sides.

She put the Master File List in the first hanging file folder in the first drawer of her filing cabinet and labeled it "Master List." She put that file tab in the center.

When she saw the brightly colored tabs standing neatly in soldier-straight rows, Eileen thought proudly, *So orderly! I know I can maintain this!*

Jeri handed Eileen a sheet with the title, "Maintaining Your Filing System." She gave Eileen a big hug, a thumbs-up, and popped out the door on her way to visit another member of her selling group.

Maintaining Your Filing System

Once you set up your filing system, it will be easy to maintain if you commit to following these steps:

Daily

- Use your Master File List when filing, adding, deleting, or moving a file from one main section to another.
- When sorting papers (including mail), jot a main category and a file name in the upper right corner. Use a sticky note if you don't want to write on the paper.
- Do all sorting at the same time, then do all filing at the same time.

Weekly

- When you leave work for the weekend, make sure your desk is clear and that your To-File pile is manageable for Monday morning. If you're not satisfied with how your office will look when you walk back into it, take time to make it look the way you want it to look when you walk back in.

Monthly

- Update your Master File List. It's easier to keep it orderly, neat, up-to-date, and even alphabetized on a computer.
- If you get backlogged, dedicate a portion of one day per month for filing. Use your birthday as a guide. (For example, if your birthday is on the seventh, use the seventh of every month as your day to file.)

Adding a File

- Consult your Master File List before creating a new file. Scan the file names to be sure you don't have a similar file listed under a different name. If it's really a new file, add the name to the master list and make a folder label using a tab in the color of that section.

Changing a File Name or File Category

- When changing a file name or category, consult the Master File List first. Cross out the old name and write in the new file name on the list, in the correct category. Make a new label with a tab of the correct color.

Deleting a File

- Cross the file name off the Master File List. Remove the plastic tab from the folder. Throw the label away.

Remember, setting up a filing system is like decorating— you never finish. You'll constantly be improving it. Expect this, and make time for it.

 FACTOID: Does getting organized make you more likely to adopt healthy habits? A study by IKEA revealed this curious relationship: 67 percent of women who color-code their files at work exercise regularly, while only 21 percent of women who have no filing system at work regularly exercise.[11]

Hans's Business File

Hans, a jolly fellow with deep dimples and a bushy white beard, was busy in his thriving real estate business. Daily filing and record keeping, along with an ever-ringing phone, kept Hans's attention perpetually divided. He knew he needed to get a handle on all the papers his office generated. *But how?* he wondered.

That's when Shirley, a new friend, introduced him to the color-coded system she used to keep her personal files in order. The same system, she promised, could help him track his plentiful documents related to closings, taxes, client files, listings, finances, and more.

At first, he doubted color-coding could really help. But after giving it some careful thought, he realized he could adapt the home filing system to handle his business files perfectly.

The "People" category could hold files on clients, prospects, vendors, and employees. "Places and Things" could contain files on tangible assets, such as furniture, computers, and vehicles. "Ideas and Interests" could hold his files related to marketing, public relations, and sales. The "Financial" section could hold his receivables and payables. "Work" could hold his administrative files.

Hans created a Master File List on his computer. This allowed him to track down papers when he needed them by simply using a search command. To make it even more efficient, he included extra key words on his list to help him locate his file. For instance, the information for his company vehicles was filed in a folder labeled "Vehicles." But when he added that name to the list, he added next to it the key words "Automobiles" and "Cars," in case he forgot what name he'd used for the file.

Smart Filing Strategies

These aren't rules, just useful suggestions. Don't fret over making sure every detail of your filing system is perfect. Chances are, you'll never look again at 80 percent of the papers you file. Just decide to work your system in whatever way helps you move forward most easily. Here are some tips that have worked well for others:

- **Separate financial papers by year.** Don't keep more than one year's worth in one folder.
- **Use a stapler, if you must attach papers to each other.** Paper clips can fall off or snag on other papers in the folder. If you must use them, attach coated paper clips to the side of the paper that will face up in the folder. That will help you spot groupings of papers and lift them out together neatly. Aluminum paper clips rust.
- **Leave enough room** for folders to move back and forth in the drawer or box. When files are packed in too tightly, it makes filing difficult and it becomes tempting to procrastinate. Remember: aim for the space to be roomy enough to fit your fist.
- **Store documents from previous tax years** in sturdy, well-labeled boxes and keep them in a dry place. In the case of an audit, papers from that year will be easy to retrieve.
- **Label file drawers clearly by category** on the front panel, making it easy for you to know at a glance where everything is filed.
- **Don't get hung up on how you write your labels.** Just make them legible. This is not the time for perfection. Remember: done is better than perfect.

Give Your Existing System a 10,000-File Tune-Up

Okay, so you may never need 10,000 files. But wouldn't it be great to know that even if you had that many, you could still find anything you needed quickly—without blowing a gasket?

Sometimes people are heavily committed to a filing system that doesn't work. Consider these candidates for a relief-bringing, 10,000-file tune-up.

File Fast? Or Well?

There are two schools of thought on filing. One suggests it's best to file in a specific place—consistently either adding to the front or back—in each folder.

The other theory is that it's best to just get the papers into the file folder quickly, and sort through them when you have time to go back.

Which one is right? Well, there's no right or wrong way. Either can be right, depending on your style.

Marsha encourages clients to file, file, file, then weed out and perfect later. It's faster and easier, and there's only a 20 percent chance you'll use the file again anyway. (Remember the Pareto Principle?) So why take time to make your files neat?

Sandra says to always add files to the front of each folder. That's the way the military does it, and following almost any rule is better than following none. The one that's right is the one that's right for you!

Dr. Marvin, an excellent dentist, also earned high marks as a file designer. The result in his filing cabinet was beautiful. Crisp manila folders poked up from neat hanging folders. The hanging files were color-coded. He even used a label maker that popped out uniform labels to be used on his hanging files instead of just printing neatly.

The problem was this: keeping his files beautifully neat claimed too much precious time. The system was too perfect. To make his system truly time-saving and useful, he needed to allow some flexibility to the rules of order he'd created.

Carol, on the other hand, had too few rules for her filing system. Each of the fourteen drawers was labeled "A–Z." She did no grouping of topics. She just alphabetized each drawer as she added to it. When she needed a document, she rarely had a clue about which drawer might hold it.

One day, in order to find the condo documents she urgently needed, she began thumbing through the front of one drawer after the next, hoping she'd find them under C for Condo.

After an extensive search, she still hadn't found the needed papers. Perhaps, she realized in alarm, it wasn't under C. Now, she wondered if she'd filed them under something else, like maybe House, Mortgage, Documents, Insurance, or something else.

Carol needed a system that worked! So did Lillian. Lillian was good at putting her papers neatly in folders and stowing them in her filing cabinet quickly, so they didn't pile up. But she didn't label the folders, and could hardly ever find them when she needed them again. This is a surprisingly common "system."

When the engine for your existing filing system begins grinding to a halt, it's time to pop open the hood and have a look—and probably time for some driver's education, as well.

But you don't toss out the car just because it needs a few repairs. As in automobiles, when it comes to filing it's important to keep what's working and fix what isn't.

If your files are labeled correctly—accurately reflecting the contents of the folder—rearranging can be done quickly. If your files are not labeled correctly, and you don't know what's in the folders, the job can be daunting. But it's well worth it, down the road.

How to Give Your Filing System a Tune-Up

Commit to using a Master File List and the five main categories we've already suggested (People, Places and Things, Ideas and Interests, Financial, and Work). Then follow these steps:

1. Gather your supplies. You'll need your Master File List; an empty file box or drawer; clear, plastic, three-inch tabs for labeling; empty hanging file folders; white filing labels; and labels in five assorted colors.

2. Transfer the papers in each file into a hanging folder. Name it and record it under the proper category on your Master File List. Label it with the color you've chosen for that category. Be sure to alternate each category's tabs to the far right or far left. Discard files you don't need.

3. Alphabetize the files within each category. Remember: the master list doesn't need to be alphabetized, because it's a living document. It changes as you add new files. Just add new file names to the bottom as you go along. They'll be easy to find within their categories, because you'll keep the files themselves alphabetized.

4. Think of the master list as your owner's manual. Store it in the first folder of the first drawer of your new filing system, which is kind of like a glove box.

If you used boxes as temporary containers, you can easily transfer the hanging files into file drawers. If you used an empty filing cabinet to create your new system, keep the now-empty cabinet right where it is, so it can be used to expand your system when necessary. Most offices can avoid paper pile-up problems simply by making more space for files.

It's So Hard to Say Good-Bye

For many of us, putting things in files is the easy part. But when we make what seems like a rational decision to get papers out of a pile by filing them, we often create a temporary solution that can become a permanent problem if left unchecked.

Being partial to making things "perfect," we don't want to make decisions about what to discard because it may end up being the wrong decision. We put things in files for one reason—we let them stay there for another reason.

Reasons to file are many. We think we might need the paper in the future. Being imaginative, we brainstorm the many ways we might use it. We think someone else might need it. We certainly don't want to miss a chance to share it. We are attracted to certain items because they're cute, funny, beautiful, etc., or because they bring back memories we're afraid we'll forget if we toss the item.

But purging files is necessary if you want your system to continue running well. In fact, like tuning up the engine benefits a car, purging files adds power to the filing system. The more you do it, and feel the freedom it gives you, the easier it gets. So how can you decide when to toss those files into the trash? As you handle each file, ask yourself these questions:

- **Do I really need it?** Ask yourself whether the contents of that file really add value to your life or work. Do you really need all of it? For example, cover sheets from faxes and memos can hit the can. Tear out the articles you wanted to save, then toss the rest of the magazine. Tear out the catalog page that shows the item you want to order, then discard the remainder.

- **Do I really want it?** A funny cartoon or something that holds significant memories may qualify to stay. But many of these things lose their appeal with time. We tend to wrap our emotions too tightly around too many items, so we need to challenge things we keep. One woman kept materials from a job she didn't like and was fired from because they represented significant years of her life. Time to let that clutter go!

- **Is it a duplicate?** If you have it in your computer, you can easily find it on the internet, or you have another copy, this item is taking up valuable room in your filing system. An assistant once was purging files and asked the boss if she could discard some records. "Yes," he said, "but make a copy before you do!" See how hard it is to let things go?

- **Is it still relevant?** Time makes some things old and unimportant. These are the easiest to discard.

- **Will I use it again?** If you will, keep it. But no matter how valuable it once was, discard it if in your best judgment you decide you won't use it again. Nobody knows the future perfectly, so responding to this question requires bold action. It's a difficult question, but it must be faced or your files will bulge with junk that obscures the papers you really will use again.

So when and how should you purge files? It's up to you, really, or your boss, or even your tax professional. But the bottom line is this: the length of stay in your filing system shouldn't be completely random. You need a system that outlines how long files of different types should stay and when they should hit the trash or shredder. Here's a guide:

- **Develop a record-retention schedule, if you don't have one.** Include your plan in the desk manual we'll describe later. If your company has specific policies for the retention of records, follow that. Tax-related files generally should be kept for seven years. But ask your accountant if your situation requires a different length of time. It can be important!
- **Schedule time to purge outdated files.** Maybe it will work for you to spend fifteen minutes doing this once or twice a week. Or maybe you'll tackle this chore once a month, or even once a year. Whatever works for you is okay. Just be sure to do it regularly—or the job will become overwhelming and daunting.
- **Label with sticky notes if you have to stop in the middle of the job.** Just put a sticky note with the date and the word "DONE" on the outside of each file drawer as you finish bringing it up-to-date. When you complete the purging chore, you can remove those notes. When you have to stop in the middle of a drawer, place a brightly colored paper as a marker to show where you quit. Write "To Here" at the top of the page.

- **Shred sensitive information** when discarding papers— things like social security numbers, credit card account numbers, bank account numbers, etc. Your commitment to security is especially important if the papers hold information from clients or other people who've trusted you. Shredders are available in a range of prices and sizes, from those that destroy one paper at a time to commercial models capable of shredding lots of paper at a time along with the staples or paper clips attached to them. There are even shredding services that will handle the job. You also could offer to return unnecessary files to the people they concern. Or archive them by removing them from your storage files to an out of the way storage area. Just be sure to keep a record of some sort about what is in each box and the range of dates involved.

Smart Steps in the Right Direction

Flip now to chapter 20, "Smart and Useful Ideas," beginning on page 207, to continue creating a powerful tool that can help you stay on track in your organizing by answering these questions:

11.1. If you haven't already, create a Master File List.

11.2. Which color label will you use for each of the categories?

11.3. As you add folders to each category, add the folder name (ideally, with key words) to the appropriate column on the master list. File the folder in the appropriate color-coded section.

11.4. Stow your Master File List in the first folder of the first drawer or box of your filing area.

Mini-Quiz

1. Is anybody complaining about the condition of your office?

2. Have you ever considered hiring outside organizing help?

3. Do you know how you would go about getting help?

If you answered "yes" to any of these, read on.

12

Reinforcements to the Rescue

Two are better than one . . . for if either of them falls,
the one will lift up his companion.

Ecclesiastes 4:9–10

Do what you do best, and delegate the rest.

Harold Taylor

Action Highlights

By the end of this chapter, you'll be prepared to:

- Tune in to your own organizational needs.
- Make the most of help from others.
- Follow standard organizing principles.
- Add a touch of beauty.
- Ask the right questions to find the perfect organizing professional for you.

Marla's office was a disaster for one specific reason—inaction. She was a magazine editor and her office was awash with query letters, proposed articles, press kits, invitations, books from authors, memos, and other flotsam that floated in.

Most didn't need to be stored. Most simply needed a decision, especially after the current month's issue was sent off to print and the next month's issue was beginning.

Next door, Richard paddled his editing kayak through challenging waters with apparent ease. From time to time, when he stood in Marla's doorway, he threatened to hire one of the professional organizers who'd been featured in their magazine. Marla's office, he reasoned, could provide fodder for a fascinating before-and-after story on office organizing. He was right.

On a whim, he compiled a list of the organizing professionals who'd been in touch with the magazine. Being a good sport, Marla agreed the before-and-after article idea might be fun, and she started investigating. She preferred hiring someone from the same city, though the magazine decision makers were willing to hire someone from out of town, if necessary. But there was more than locale to consider.

Marla considered the organizers' qualifications. Most on the list belonged to the National Association of Professional Organizers (NAPO). The group's website included ways to locate the right candidate by specialty and by location from a membership of more than four thousand.

She learned that some NAPO members were part of the National Study Group on Chronic Disorganization (NSGCD), which trains professionals to deal with the messiest of clients. (Marla suspected that this might be the group for her.)

Some Christian professionals belonged to a group called Faithful Organizers. She even discovered a group called Professional Organizers of Canada (POC).

Choosing a Rescuer

Having conducted searches for doctors, handymen, and nannies, Marla knew the basics of checking out qualifications and asking for references. She prepared some questions then called her top three candidates, making notes as they chatted.

Even though it was "just business," Marla was surprised at how vulnerable she felt when she considered letting someone else into the inner workings of her office. It was embarrassing to admit she wasn't able to control her work, as Richard and her other colleagues did. She listened for acceptance and reassurance from the organizers she interviewed.

After phoning the three who seemed most promising, Marla chose Charlene, an experienced organizer with glowing references. But what really sold her were two things: Charlene seemed to know her stuff, giving solid answers that really made sense as they talked. And, even more importantly, she seemed to really listen and be empathetic to Marla's problem. *Whoopee!* thought Marla. *Help is on the way. Great!*

To her colleagues, Marla only mentioned coolly, "I believe this might make an interesting article."

"Perhaps so," they answered just as casually. Then they whispered together, "Whoopee! Help is on the way. Great!"

Gearing Up

Charlene had made a phone assessment of Marla's problem, and it seemed clear to her that, among other things, Marla's office suffered from many problems common in offices. One was a lack of proper furniture that would allow Marla to comfortably and conveniently do her job.

Administrators making furniture selections often overlook the importance of adequate tools for office work. They're focused on hiring highly qualified people for good salaries—and then they often send them to poorly equipped workstations. Like the miller's daughter in the fairy tale *Rumpelstiltskin,* highly paid professionals are often sent to ill-equipped offices and expected to spin gold from straw.

Often, the employee must take the initiative to try to obtain the needed furniture pieces. In a large company, the maintenance staff can be powerful allies in this mission.

Home offices often suffer from the same malady. Because furniture seems so mundane compared to the focus of business plans, its importance is easy to overlook. But setting up a workstation with adequate storage and a convenient flow is crucial.

Good workflow is accomplished by setting up a rational plan to move documents (or projects) forward one step at a time in the easiest way possible. Deliberate thought about the placement of furniture will facilitate smooth movement.

Marla sent a few digital pictures of her topsy-turvy office to Charlene and discussed with her what she needed. From Charlene's experience, it was clear to her what was missing. So at her direction, Marla's first task was to obtain a large bookcase, a collection of baskets or bins that would fit on the bookcase shelves, a two-drawer filing cabinet, two open-top crates for handling files, a larger wastebasket, and a bigger desk. She also needed a package of white storage boxes. She already had a usable credenza.

The Big Day

Marla liked Charlene right away. She was upbeat and all business. She also was dressed in red, Marla's favorite color, which gave Charlene a look of confidence.

Getting right to work, Charlene made a quick sketch of how Marla's new furniture would be arranged and what each piece would hold.

Within minutes, it became apparent that furniture was not Marla's biggest problem. The problem was she didn't make

What's the Cost to Hire Professional Help?

Most organizers charge by the hour. Some charge by the day or by the project.

The rate usually is based on the organizer's level of experience, the area of the country, and the type of service being provided. On average, hourly rates for professional organizers in the United States are between $55 and $150 an hour.

Before hiring an organizer, consider asking candidates these questions:

- How long have you been in the organizing business?
- Are you a member of NAPO? If so, since when?
- Do you have any experience with organizing areas such as chronic disorganization, coaching, time management, interior design, feng shui, or home staging?
- What is your specialty or particular area of expertise?
- What kinds of organizing projects have you done?
- Who is your typical client?
- Will you describe your organizing process/approach? (For example, consulting, coaching, hands-on, team organizing, seminars/workshops, training, etc.)
- What is your fee structure and cancellation policy?
- Can you provide references?
- I've tried to get organized before. How will this be different?

good or quick organizing decisions, probably because she hadn't set up good systems to guide her.

As they worked together, they chatted comfortably about Marla's needs. Charlene's philosophy was that she was primarily organizing the individual, not the office, so she wanted to know Marla better.

To start getting control, they began the first logical step: the sorting process. They set up a few boxes and labeled them with the chief categories that represented most of Marla's materials—"Layouts of Upcoming Issues," "Articles," "Queries," "Press Kits," "Free Samples," "DVDs and Videos,"

"Meeting Notes," "Invitations," and "Memos." They made a Master Theme List of those categories and tacked it to Marla's bulletin board.

"We'll start by clearing the floor, because it's the largest surface, and we'll move upward from there," Charlene explained, as they began sorting the jumble into the boxes. "It's important first to get all of your surfaces clear."

As they grouped her items, Marla was surprised to see how they naturally fell into so few categories. What had seemed overwhelming and confusing began to seem manageable. She began to have hope that she could create lasting order in her office.

After forty minutes, they were able to move up from the floor to the chair seat, the desk, and the credenza. They sorted most items and papers into boxes. They stowed books on the bookcase to be grouped by subject later. They tossed useless papers and items into the new large trash can. Every half hour or so, a photographer would pop in to record the progress, and a writer stopped by frequently, jotting down details in her reporter's notebook.

Once everything had been collected into boxes, it was clear how much room was needed to stow each category. They set up bins on the bookshelves labeled "Press Kits," "DVDs and Videos," "Samples," and "Miscellaneous." Those items were moved from the white boxes to their new homes and neatly stowed.

On the credenza, Charlene put two open-top crates for hanging files, which would hold a To-Do Action File. She also put a large bin on one end of the credenza to receive incoming mail. And she instructed Marla to try to handle the mail as soon as possible after delivery each day.

Marla's desk held her computer and phone. Nothing else. She wanted to keep it clear.

Some organized types can tolerate a few things out of place. But once people like Marla start letting a few things leak out of place, the whole system of order falls apart. The clutter-free desk was an inspiration to her, and a reminder of her new way of life. The printer, fax, and corporate files she'd previously kept on her desk were relocated to a common area outside her office.

Next, Marla and Charlene needed to transfer items in the categorized boxes to their designated storage areas. They stashed bulkier items—clipboards, whiteboard erasers, and notebooks—in bins and put them on bookcase shelves. They filed papers into a To-Do Action File under categories: "Queries," "Articles," "Meeting Notes," and "Invitations."

They filed the reference papers she needed in the new two-drawer filing cabinet. With a grin, Marla hung a "Smile, God loves you" sign she'd recovered from the mess.

As they emptied the boxes, they collapsed them back into their original flat shape. The photographer documented their disappearance, along with the growing order in Marla's formerly out-of-control office.

Finishing Touches

"There's still something missing," Charlene mused, when they were finished. "Where's the beauty? We always need a spot of beauty to keep us inspired. Woman does not succeed by order alone, you know."

So, with permission, Marla confiscated a picture of a Florida beach scene from the hallway and hung it directly in front of her desk.

It had been a long but wonderful ten-hour day. The pictures for the article revealed the makeover miracle. And later, the story showed step-by-step how the transformation happened. The final picture of Marla's beaming face as she stood in her renewed office said it all. Marla's office was now under control and had been transformed into a beautiful and businesslike place to work.

Even Richard and Marla's other co-workers were impressed. Everyone in the office admired the gift of order Charlene had helped Marla create for herself. Marla, ultimately, had to be the one making the decisions throughout the project. But Charlene's magical skills sparked changes worthy of a celebration.

Gathering up her purse and briefcase, Charlene gave Marla hearty congratulations and promised to be available by phone for any questions that she had.

"Remember to keep the trash can close by, keep the desk clear, and use the last fifteen minutes of each day to tidy up," she said with a smile. "Until you get in the habit of staying organized, email me each day and let me know how you're doing."

Then, like Santa, with a quick nod she was gone.

 FACTOID: The top reasons NAPO members have been hired to organize companies or offices that aren't home-based: (1) Improve general employee productivity, (2) Maximize office space, (3) Assist specific employees needing organizational skills, (4) Shelving and storage solutions, and (5) Preparation to move the company.[12]

Sometimes, a push in the right direction from a knowledgeable professional is all you need. Consider this glowing report an organizer's assistant gave her, after following up with a client who'd hired them for a consultation and then followed the recommendations on her own—with exciting results:

Yesterday, I followed up with a call to the advertising sales manager in the newspaper office. She blew me away! She was excited! She bought a nice, vertical, four-drawer filing cabinet at a flea market and put all the right stuff in it. She filed every single piece of paper in her office—in color-coded files! She has a master list. Her expenses, including the filing cabinet, were just under $150. She plans to buy a two-drawer file and add it in.

Her office looks amazing, she says, and is totally organized! She turned her desk drawer files around to face her. She said, "I know every single paper in this office is in a file and I know exactly where it is!"

She'd even taken handwritten business notes off the wall and typed them up! Then gave them a file! She said that having the tools is all it took.

She began Saturday afternoon and spent six hours, then spent eleven more on Sunday and left at 1:30 a.m. feeling like a conqueror!

She said you are marvelous, and she is happier than she's been in a long time and feeling ever so free. Her boss wanted to know who had helped her.

Later, her car broke down and had to go to the shop. She had to clean it out, as well. She said she "couldn't even fit a toothpick into the trunk." She emptied the stuff into her office and dealt with that stuff, also. Now, the car's all nice and organized too.

Next she will attempt to de-clutter her bedroom, because she now has so much more energy she has to find something new to do with it. She can't wait! Her energy almost knocked me over the way it was pouring through the phone!

Don't Overlook Kid Power

Professional organizers aren't the only ones who can offer assistance. Certain friends (understanding ones), household employees, and savvy young people seeking extra money can be good sources of help. In fact, they were the go-to resource before the organizing profession formally took shape in the 1980s.

Take the example of Rochelle. She wasn't truly the disorganized type, but she was floundering in the management of her new home office. Unfortunately, she didn't have a friend with lots of organizing experience and she couldn't afford to hire a professional. So Rochelle contacted a responsible high school senior and offered her a job as an office helper. Sure enough, Vie was available.

One Saturday morning, Rochelle put on her boss's hat and worked with Vie on organizing the space for her new business selling homegrown, organic vegetables out of her garage. Having three hours set aside for the task and an eager face waiting for instruction helped Rochelle think clearly about what needed to be done. She quickly realized that the key was to simply make decisions about where things should go . . . then put them there!

For three Saturday mornings, she and Vie worked on filing, purging, moving files, and bringing Rochelle's Master File List up-to-date. Though only seventeen years old, Vie was a surprisingly competent organizer. She'd gained valuable experience and a strong set of organizing skills, she admitted, by helping her mother stay organized at home.

Every few weeks after that, Vie returned for a morning of catch-up organizing. When she went away to college to study international business, she left the names of two more teens who could replace her. Having an affordable helper met Rochelle's need well for several years.

Smart Steps in the Right Direction

Flip now to chapter 20, "Smart and Useful Ideas," beginning on page 207, to continue creating a powerful tool that can help you stay on track in your organizing by answering these questions:

12.1. If you're considering hiring a professional organizer, make a list of questions you'd like to ask candidates for the job.

12.2. Compile a list of potential organizers.

12.3. Schedule a time to call your top candidates and set up interviews with them.

12.4. If you'd like to enlist the help of a friend or youth, write the names of a few you could ask about sharing the job with you. How much would you be willing to pay for help?

Mini-Quiz

1. Do you have a satisfactory place at home for personal business?

2. Do you do office work outside of your regular office setup?

3. Have you made adequate preparation if you travel with office work?

If you travel with office work, or if you do additional work outside your office and you haven't stopped to consider how to make it easier, check out what follows.

13

The Nontraditional Office

How can I think outside the box when I work inside
a cube?

Unknown

Action Highlights

By the end of this chapter, you'll be prepared to:

- Set up your car as a rolling office.
- Create an adequate office in an unusually small space.
- Solve home-based office woes.
- Organize your briefcase to work for you.
- Upgrade your office's look and feel.

Offices come in many forms. Some are solidly based in a
building. Others are totally on the go.

Jobs like Carla's require a portable setup to move seam-
lessly from the seat of a car, through an airport, and into

the friendly skies. Selling radio advertising spots requires her to call on clients in person all over the country. And Carla's income depends on her ability to work quickly and efficiently. Her GPS gets her to destinations without fail, but what really makes her productive is the small officelike environment she's created in her car.

Managing client files on the run is key to her success. She keeps well-organized folders with contracts and promotional materials neatly filed in crates attached with Velcro to the carpet in her car trunk.

Another helpful innovation is a small desktop that clips onto her steering wheel. (When she's parked, of course!) It allows her to fill out contracts on a stable surface, supports her laptop, and even holds her lunch. Her glove compartment functions as a desk drawer, tidily corralling pens, tape, paper clips, rubber bands, a stapler, and other supplies. Although many car organizing products are available online and in stores, Carla found she could adapt items from her home office, such as the desk organizer she cut down to hold items in the glove compartment.

She stowed jumper cables, a flashlight with extra batteries, a small first aid kit, and an ice scraper in a plastic box labeled "Emergency" tucked next to the file crates in her trunk.

She's especially proud of an automotive maintenance binder that fits into a compartment in one of her filing crates. Gas expenses, emergency car repairs, and regular maintenance are recorded in the book, along with all related receipts. That helps make end-of-the-year tax preparation a snap for Carla.

Her rolling office is easy to keep neat, and a breeze to use. She's always ready to go.

Neatness Counts

Becoming a cosmetics distributor taxed Marilyn's organizational abilities to the max. She'd gotten lazy about keeping the kids under control in the car, so clothes, shoes, empty plastic cups, receipts, fliers, food wrappers, and other unattended debris filled every cranny.

Marilyn knew that, from time to time, customers peered into her car as she reached in for a brochure or a product. The thought of that made her cringe. To make matters worse, she was aware that her sponsor kept her vehicle in pristine condition. Change was mandatory.

So Marilyn made a plan. She toted three boxes out to her driveway and labeled them "House," "Trash," and "Car." She rustled up the kids and put them to work emptying the car. Most of what they pulled out was trash. What didn't belong back in the car, they took into the house.

Marilyn then evaluated her car space. There were three areas for storage: the glove compartment, the side pockets, and the trunk. In the glove compartment, she decided to keep the car manual, insurance papers and registration, and an ice scraper. She was also able to fit in a small flashlight and a box of adhesive bandages. Although she had a GPS, she stuck in a map for help when she needed an overview of her travels.

In the car's side pockets, she stowed a coupon organizer, a notepad, and pens. In the trunk, she placed three cardboard boxes. She labeled the first box "Emergency," and put in jumper cables, some flares, a roll of paper towel, duct tape, extra windshield wiper fluid, a comfortable pair of old walking shoes, and some emergency cash. The box labeled "Dry Cleaner" would carry garments that needed to be cleaned. The third was labeled "Charity" to hold items she planned to donate.

Marilyn's home office was her base. But when on the go, she decided to use a large company bag to carry products and a briefcase to hold business-related papers such as brochures, her calendar, lists, and notes about leads. And when she returned home from business outings, she now made a habit of syncing all new information from her Smartphone to her home office computer.

Then she tackled her biggest challenge: breaking the habit she and her kids had of letting clutter pile up in the car. To combat that, she stashed plastic grocery bags under her front seat and encouraged the kids to use them to carry in trash every time they got out of the car at the house. "Feed Mr. Trash Can!" became their slogan whenever they pulled up to a store that had a trash bin out front.

Having an organized setup and plan for maintaining it allowed Marilyn to keep her car neat and her business moving forward.

A Just-Plane-Perfect Office

A professional speaker, Warren traveled mostly by plane and his briefcase was his office-in-a-box. Inside, he had folders for works in progress, speeches, handouts, itineraries, and more.

Each item was in a color-coded file. He used a red folder for his speeches and notes, a blue folder for articles he was currently writing, a green folder for his handouts, and a yellow folder for his itinerary. This way, at a glance, Warren could be sure he had everything he needed prior to leaving his office.

Personal issues that required his attention while he was traveling had their own folder, as well. His briefcase was well suited to his needs, and held his laptop computer securely, with easy access through a zippered flap.

By keeping everything in order as he went, he could get things accomplished whenever he had a few moments of downtime. That meant less catching up to do when he got home, and much more time to spend with his family.

The Cubbyhole Office

Some "offices" aren't offices at all. These ultrasmall spaces would be better called "areas designated for office-type work."

Put Your Briefcase to Work for You

A messy or inadequate briefcase can make your job harder than it has to be, but a well-organized design can lighten your load. Put your briefcase to work for you by:

- **Asking the tough question,** "Is my current briefcase really right for me?" Maybe it's too big, too small, too hard to access, or too old. If so, go shopping guilt-free and get what you need with features that will make your work easier.
- **Plan for where specific files go.** Choose to organize by date, urgency, subject, priority, or whatever works for you—then stick with that plan. Put the most-used folders near the front.
- **Label manila folders boldly** or use labeled folders of different colors to help you spot what you need at a glance.
- **Tuck in a few empty envelopes** for collecting receipts.
- **Put items in their proper places as you go,** rather than just stuffing things in and vowing to sort them out later. Stick to your system and you'll reap rewards. Filing later is a frustrating activity, because the pile becomes more unmanageable as it grows larger and as your recollection of the papers' importance fades.
- **Schedule a regular time to reorganize** your briefcase. Usually, the best time is shortly after returning from your trip.

In a place of business, this type of workspace contains little more than a desk—or some other kind of flat surface—and maybe a filing cabinet. In homes, it might be a catch-as-catch-can affair, perhaps a countertop or folding table.

In a recent survey, about half of all businesses were home-based, amounting to about sixteen million total, according to the Small Business Administration. But at-home entrepreneurs aren't the only ones needing home-based working space. In the corporate world, about five million employees work from home most of the time, and another seven million do so at least once a month. That's about twenty-eight million people conducting all or part of their business activities from home. And these numbers are rising rapidly.

Some of these at-home workers have carved out traditional offices, but many others must find a spot in an already crowded home environment.

Whether yours is a cubbyhole office in a home or a limited space at a business, it's imperative to set up a practical way of working in the space you have. To make the most of the space you have:

- Restrict the materials you get out only to what you can handle at one time.
- Use your working surface for activity only, not as a holding area for materials that need to be put away.
- Store often-used things at arm's length, and keep seldom-used tools elsewhere.
- Have a place for everything and keep everything in its place. This principle masquerades as a trite old rule for prim elderly ladies. But in reality, it's one of the top powerhouse principles in the organizing process.
- Display a sign that says "Stow As You Go" until you make that a habit.
- Clear your work surface at the end of every day, or at least stack visible items neatly.

Working with Limited Space

Phyllis worked from home as a customer service representative for a large company. Her "office" was her kitchen counter, where she set up her laptop. She wore headphones to answer her constantly ringing telephone. Occasionally, depending on the nature of the current call, she was able to move around the house for a bit of exercise or a little housework. The secret of her organizational success was that she kept all of her materials in order in one place, and she promptly stored them at the end of her workday.

Juan's tiny efficiency apartment in Manhattan had no room for an office for his freelance writing business. So when he was working, he pulled out a folding card table from behind the sofa, flipped open his briefcase, and powered up his laptop computer. He loved that his job put him right in the middle of the action he was observing for a story. Having a pop-open office worked in his small space because he resisted the temptation to leave the table up and use it for storage. His unbreakable rule: put the table behind the sofa and any stray papers back into his briefcase the moment he finished writing. Only the laptop was allowed to remain in view, in case he needed it for a spur-of-the-moment idea.

School administrators gave Rebecca, an itinerant speech pathologist who travels from school to school, the only space their crowded elementary could spare—a broom closet! To make it suitable for meeting with students, she cleared it out and turned it into a cozy, workable space. She commandeered a rolling cart, which she used each night to carry home her records, equipment, and books she used with the children. The melding of the cart and the closet created a workable office.

Brandon, a corporate executive, conducted business as he spent the winter in Florida. He neither wanted nor needed a full-sized office. In his living area sat a large armoire that, when opened, revealed a capsule office, complete with pull-out desktop, file drawer, shelves, drawers, and lighting. His business phone line snaked in through the back with other electronic cables. A furniture catalog would call it a computer armoire. But the truth is, it nicely accommodated the basics of a complete (but very small) office.

Because his "office" wasn't equipped with a copier, he simply visited a local business service center at a nearby office store when necessary.

Solutions for Home Office Woes

Most office problems have to do with handling paper, but that's not always the case.

Sometimes, especially in offices in the home, problems arise from not-so-obvious troublemakers. Consider whether these tiny tweaks or sneaky solutions could assuage your office woes:

- **Upgrade your office's look.** If it's looking dreary, invest in new paint in an energizing color or some updated flooring. Research on colors has shown red increases attention to detail, while blue stimulates creativity.
- **Air out problems.** Studies show that poor air quality lowers productivity of office workers. Mindfully opening windows, running fans, or changing air filters will help.
- **Cool it.** Research revealed that when the air temperature is at 77 degrees, workers increased the amount of productivity and accuracy of their work. Too cold or hot decreases output and quality of work.
- **Go solo.** If your office shares space with exercise equipment, hobby supplies, or guest furniture, try to kick out those intruders. Having a clear separation of work and personal space is helpful for a healthy work-life balance. Having a dedicated office will allow you to set it up in a way that makes it most comfortable for your working hours.

The Bottom Line

In today's complex world, overrun by personal and business paperwork, an office of some kind is a necessity for just about everyone. People in today's paper-driven world are beginning to embrace the fact that they need to set up their own personal office in the home, even if it's just for running the household.

In planning your space at home or on the go, consider what's worked for others and determine what's right for you. If space seems sorely lacking, try creating an office under a stairwell, in an emptied coat closet, or behind a screen in a

- **Silence distractions.** Barking dogs, the family TV, or a teen's reverberating music can make it almost impossible to concentrate. Don't ignore the problem. Take charge and make adjustments where possible. Move the dog, modify the habits, or change the location of the noisy family members.
- **Let there be light!** Poor lighting is not just unpleasant, it can be damaging to your eyes. Overhead general lighting brightens the room, while "directed lighting" is suggested for specific jobs. Care is required to keep glare off the computer screen.
- **Halt interruptions.** Frequent interruptions from family must be stopped. Try making your request for uninterrupted work time a little clearer with visual or audible cues. For example, you might say, "Please don't interrupt me for an hour. I will set this timer," or "When the door is closed, pretend I'm out of the house." You might tack this reminder on your office door: "Lack of preparation on your part does not constitute an emergency on my part." Preparing ahead for family needs and care before you enter the office will enable you to work with fewer interruptions.
- **Take a parenting break.** While you're working in your home office, it probably will be impossible to supervise small children closely. Consider bringing in someone who can be responsible for the children, or take them to a child-care facility.

corner. Use your imagination! Just remember, the key is setting up your small space in a way that works for you, then straightening it as soon as your work there is done. Or at least, when you leave your work for the day, contain and disguise it.

 FACTOID: In a Greenfield Online survey of 2,611 office workers, 55 percent of US respondents said they have an office at home.[13]

Smart Steps in the Right Direction

Flip now to chapter 20, "Smart and Useful Ideas," beginning on page 207, to continue creating a powerful tool that can help you stay on track in your organizing by answering these questions:

13.1. Do you need an on-the-go office? If so, write which strategies from this chapter would work well for you.

13.2. Which techniques could you use to create a well-set-up cubbyhole office?

13.3. Do you need to set up office space in your home? Where will you do that? And what supplies do you need to outfit it appropriately for the space you have and the jobs you need to do there?

Mini-Quiz

1. Do you perceive time management to be a significant difficulty in your work?

2. Are you good at delegating?

3. Do you spend too much time solving unexpected problems?

If you answered "yes" to numbers 1 and 3 and "no" to number 2, the next chapter will help you gain control of how you use your time.

14

Where Did the Day Go?

If you chase two rabbits, both will escape.
Chinese proverb

Action Highlights

By the end of this chapter, you'll be prepared to:

- Accurately assess your present usage of time.
- Create a helpful time-use chart.
- Decide on jobs to delegate.

Time management is not the art of getting everything done. It is the art of getting the most important things done. So time management really is the art of skillfully managing priorities.

At the heart of time management is planning and self-control. If you can stand solidly on those two legs, you'll be successful. The old saying sums it up well: plan your work, and work your plan. We'll help you learn how.

Ana Gets Time-Wise

With long black hair and a winning smile, Ana fit in well with her exotic work environment, researching microbiology in a makeshift office in the jungles of Africa.

But as hard as she worked, she was producing far less than she'd hoped. At just twenty-one years old, she already had a highly developed sense of responsibility toward her work. She wanted to show her academic abilities. But most of all, she wanted to make discoveries that would benefit villagers whose health was threatened by the subject of her study, the tsetse fly.

However, the work didn't flow as smoothly as she'd hoped. As Ana transitioned between the field, where she conducted surveys and experiments, and the office (such as it was) where she prepared her reports, her paperwork became hard to manage.

She struggled with missed deadlines for reports, incomplete information, and flawed findings. She knew she could do the work. But somehow, she always seemed to be falling further behind.

She took some time to think about the root of the problem, and decided that the culprits were her cluttered office and poor time management. She also realized that clutter can be caused by the poor management of time, and that time management problems sometimes stem from having too much clutter. She decided to try to get control of her time management problem first.

Being a scientist, Ana naturally analyzed her problem and looked for possible solutions. She thought back to times she'd successfully used a diet log to manage her weight and a money log to bring her finances under control. A time log of her working hours surely would help her too, she decided.

Using a time log divided into half-hour increments, she kept track of everything for three days. Then she reviewed

Ana's Time Log   Day_____ Date _____

6:00 a.m.	
6:30	
7:00	
7:30	
8:00	Daily meeting with team
8:30	Daily meeting with team
9:00	Unassigned
9:30	Unassigned
10:00	Unassigned
10:30	Unassigned
11:00	Evaluate articles
11:30	Evaluate articles
12:00 p.m.	Lunch
12:30	Lunch
1:00	Meeting with community leaders
1:30	Meeting with community leaders
2:00	Scientific study
2:30	Scientific study
3:00	Scientific study
3:30	Scientific study
4:00	Treatment options
4:30	Treatment options
5:00	Time to go home
5:30	
6:00	
6:30	
7:00	
7:30	
8:00	
8:30	

Where does your time go? Track it daily for one week and see.

Time Log   Day_____ Date _____

6:00 a.m.

6:30

7:00

7:30

8:00

8:30

9:00

9:30

10:00

10:30

11:00

11:30

12:00 p.m.

12:30

1:00

1:30

2:00

2:30

3:00

3:30

4:00

4:30

5:00

5:30

6:00

6:30

7:00

7:30

8:00

8:30

Where does your time go? Track it daily for one week and see.

the log, noting time spent on working in the field, doing office work, studying, traveling, and handling personal affairs (such as eating, taking breaks, visiting with colleagues). This gave her a clear view of where her time had been going.

Where does your time go? Track it daily for one week and see. Use the blank time log provided to chart the way you spend *your* day.

If you often wonder, "Where did the day go?" when you stare at a list of unfinished tasks, try tracking your time. Then evaluate where it is spent. We guarantee you'll find some surprises: you waste more time than you thought, activities take longer than you'd anticipated, and interruptions happen more frequently than you'd realized.

When Ana evaluated her time log, she was able to make significant changes by grouping activities and cutting out interruptions over which she had some control. She realized she had less time than she thought and began guarding her minutes more carefully.

When keeping your log, tune in to feelings of when your energy is at its peak and note that on your log. Some people are definitely morning people. We call them Larks. Some people are Owls, who really come alive in the evening.

Keep your log carefully for three or more days. Getting a clear picture of how you spend your time is the first step toward using it more wisely in the future.

Optimizing Work Hours

After tracking your time, you should have a good idea of the times each week required for specific activities such as regular appointments and meetings, mealtimes, travel time, and such. Highlight those hours. What's left is the time available for other things.

Like Ana, you may be surprised at how little time can be

allotted for important activities. But at least now you can be realistic about how much time you truly have left to accomplish what you want to do.

As much as you can, plan to tackle big jobs when you're at your most alert and energetic. High-energy times are best for office organizing projects. Routine jobs can be scheduled for when your creative juices start slowing to a trickle. Until you perk up, cut yourself some slack by planning to do mundane tasks like straightening your desk drawer or sharpening pencils.

In planning your workdays, keep your goals and priorities in mind. To do that well, it's important to clarify what they are. This sounds obvious, but it's true. If you fail to clearly identify your goals and priorities, you'll probably end up wondering why you're not progressing.

So make a list. Some activities on your schedule will be constants; others will change from time to time. Write them down and post them close to your desk so they won't be overlooked as you create your work plan. Using your original time log, look for similar tasks that could be scheduled together to save time.

Ana had a few consistent tasks that were required, including performing scientific studies on the incidence of dengue fever, reviewing articles, finding new treatment options, and attending meetings to determine ways to make current treatments available to impoverished people. Once she put those big jobs on her time management plan, she found room for lower priority jobs as well.

As she examined her time management plan and thought about the many jobs listed there, she realized there was one big gun she wasn't using effectively in her battle to manage her time: delegating tasks! She wasn't managing her assistant or other office members effectively. Once she identified jobs she was doing that could be delegated, she set about finding others who could do them.

How to Delegate with Success

To delegate effectively, you need to:

- Make sure the person understands exactly what you want him or her to do. Write out instructions, if necessary.
- Choose the right candidate for the job. Double-check that the person you assign to the job is actually trained to do it.
- Set deadlines. Check in regularly to ensure the job's being done properly, especially if it's freshly delegated.
- Give the person you select for the job the authority to carry it out.
- Evaluate how well the job was done, when it's complete, and offer praise, along with any pointers for doing better the next time.

When Ana began delegating, she found it to be one of her most beneficial time management changes. Individuals who manage their businesses solo need to remember this: there probably are tasks that are important but don't generate revenue, such as bookkeeping and filing. Jobs like this, which are time-consuming but not integral to the success of the business, often can be done by a part-time assistant or even a retailer that offers business support services.

Making Your Own Weapon of Mass Production

There's a Chinese proverb that says it all: "The faintest ink is more powerful than the strongest memory." Translation: Trying to keep everything in your head is a lot of work and a method proven to be unreliable. Don't work so hard. Be productively lazy. Write it down! You'll be amazed at how much relief this method gives you—and how efficient it makes you.

The first step is to create a Master To-Do List. It will list everything you want to accomplish.

Some people keep a list like this in a desk drawer, in a binder, on a Smartphone, in a computer file, or posted on the wall. Ana tacked hers on a bulletin board for easy access as other ideas bubbled to the surface.

This list doesn't have to be fancy, but it's very important—it keeps your long-term goals in sight. Otherwise, they may fade in your memory.

Describe your "Important but Not Urgent" items here. You may not address them anytime soon, but at least you won't forget them.

After you've created your Master To-Do List, you can create your daily To-Do list, using our old friend, grouping. Fold a piece of paper in half one way and then the other to create four even squares. Label each quadrant with a word that makes sense in light of your activities, such as: "Go," "Call," "Do," and "Write" or "Buy." The first three are good choices for most people, but the fourth square can be customized to meet your individual circumstances.

Go	**Call**
Do	**Buy**

These groupings are related to the location of where you do the jobs. In the "Go" box, list places you need to go to accomplish your tasks. Under "Call," list people you need to contact by phone. Under "Do," list other things that must be accomplished in the office, and in the last box, list everything else. Occasionally other listings apply more directly to your situation; your quadrants might change to categories like "Speaking," "Assistant," "Meetings," and "Office Work."

Remember, appointments go on the planner. The To-Do list is for items that don't have a scheduled time to be completed. Next to each entry on the list, draw a small box. Put check marks in the boxes as you accomplish your tasks.

To make your list even more powerful, include a guess as to how long each activity will take. That will help you spot opportunities to work them into your time management plan. In addition, include an important detail or two about each task, such as where a needed file is located or the phone number for the call you need to make.

If you find that you have a handful of tasks listed in each quadrant, pick three to five that are your priorities for the day and put a star or asterisk beside each. To emphasize your priorities even further, write three to five of your To-Do tasks in bold marker on a separate piece of paper and put it in a place where you'll see it throughout the day, maybe on a clipboard, on a bulletin board, or under the mug on your desk.

Follow this plan, and you will have created a weapon of mass production!

Six Good Reasons to Write Out Your To-Do List

Some people don't use a To-Do list because they think that creating one long list of tasks will be too daunting and confusing—a major time-waster—and they prefer to spend their time "doing" instead of "writing," they say.

People who become more productive, efficient, and less

stressed after beginning to use a To-Do list agree that it helps them to:

- **Remember important tasks.** Using your memory is great as long as it's working great. But the moment you get overwhelmed and forget something, your entire strategy falls apart like a house of cards.
- **Prioritize** what needs to be done first. Sometimes having the list in front of you helps you to see the big picture.
- **Think creatively,** because the mind is freer. Instead of using it to store mundane tasks, you can use your brain-power to solve problems and create.
- **Schedule effectively.** When everything is listed, it's easier to see priorities and get things done in the most effective order.
- **Organize thoughts.** Writing the list down gives you an overview of what needs to be done and helps you plan.
- **Diffuse stress.** Writing down what needs to be done removes the worry that you'll forget something important.

After You Make the Plan, Work the Plan

Once Ana created a purposeful plan on paper for using her time, she test-drove it to see if it really fit her needs. She continued tweaking it until she found a balance that worked for her.

Whether you work in a corporate setting, at home, or in a makeshift office in Africa, working the plan isn't always easy. Interruptions can throw you off course.

There are two kinds of interruptions: internal and external. Internal interruptions come from character issues, such as perfectionism and procrastination. The external ones come from people or activities in our lives such as family, co-workers, phones, texts, and more. Whatever their type, letting interruptions run rampant will do serious damage to your time management plan.

Smart Time Management Tricks

People who are particularly good at managing their time efficiently don't just use a planner and a To-Do list—they also:

- **Create uninterrupted time,** either by scheduling "closed door" time, or trading off with another worker to cover phones, etc.
- **Prioritize To-Do list** activities with numbers or letters. Hint: It helps to place a star by the day's top item of importance.
- **Finish one job before starting another.**
- **Schedule wisely,** planning not just for an activity but also for the preparation, completion, and any necessary follow-up.
- **Stay on task,** not letting distractions pull them away from what they're supposed to be doing.
- **Delegate** whenever possible.
- **Gather materials** for a project before beginning.
- **Set aside their "best" time of day** for jobs that require the most concentration.
- **Say no** to requests that would overbook them.
- **Refuse to procrastinate,** and push ahead bravely to accomplish their least pleasant tasks before they become overdue.
- **Track and eliminate time-wasters** and chronic distractions.
- **Note all appointments** faithfully so they can be reviewed on the calendar at any time.
- **Set goals and post them** where they can be seen.
- **Prioritize tasks** daily, and make adjustments as circumstances change.
- **Set false deadlines** for themselves, so they'll be less likely to be late.
- **Minimize interruptions** by putting specific strategies in place.

Interrupting the Flow of Interruptions

You may feel like screaming when faced with one interruption after the next: unexpected visitors, phone calls, emergencies.

You can manage them more politely and effectively—and keep your time management plan on track—if you:

- **Face your desk away from the door.** Eye contact is an invitation to interrupt!
- **Stand up, and remain standing,** if someone comes into your office. That sends the subtle hint they shouldn't settle in and stay too long.
- **Remove interruption magnets**—candy, tissues, or supplies. To keep unwanted visitors from dropping in for these, stow them out of sight.
- **Position a clock in an obvious place** so both you and your visitor will be more fully aware of the time being used.
- **Schedule a regular time to meet** with people who need to speak with you often. That should reduce the number of pop-in visits.
- **Offer to schedule a time to meet** with someone who drops by when you're busy. That may be the hint they need to call first before making an unexpected visit.
- **Use voice mail or an answering machine** to take phone messages, then schedule a time to return calls.
- **Clue people in about your availability with subtle hints.** Say things like, "Sure, I can talk for just a minute."

Smart Steps in the Right Direction

Flip now to chapter 20, "Smart and Useful Ideas," beginning on page 207, to continue creating a powerful tool that can help you stay on track in your organizing by answering these questions:

14.1. Make a copy of the time log on page 161 and record how your time is spent during the week.

When You Are Your Own Worst Enemy

Sometimes, we do things to sabotage our own progress on a project. Instead of tackling what needs to be done, we resolve to make just one more phone call, get some advice from a co-worker, check our email, or even just take a water break. We tell ourselves that we want to get these things out of the way before we buckle down to work, but the reality is we're wasting precious time.

These sneaky little time-wasters are games we play with ourselves. A little bit of perfectionism plays a part here, as does procrastination. Be alert to these sly, self-induced time-wasters, or they'll suck the energy from your productivity.

Your time log will help you spot these creeping into your daily work—that "quick" call to your friend to see what she's having for dinner; that game of solitaire to give yourself a mental break; a decision to stop and plan more, rather than pushing ahead with necessary work; stopping to read "just a few" pages of your novel; doing "a bit" of web surfing; checking your cell phone for missed calls; confirming your hair appointment; refreshing your coffee.

Anything you do just before you get down to business on that hard thing you really don't want to do is probably a sneaky little time-waster. We embrace them because they give us an excuse to postpone jobs we really don't want to do. But in truth, they're interruptions that must be avoided if we're to remain organized and productive.

14.2. Block out all of the precommitted time during your work-week. Note how much time you actually have available to accomplish other things you want to do.

14.3. List steps you plan to take in order to improve your time management.

14.4. Create a Master To-Do List and a daily To-Do list.

Maybe boredom, an abundance of unpleasant jobs, or your habit of procrastinating keeps you from using your time effectively. Or maybe your desire to be perfect at everything you do is keeping you from moving forward, because you're unwilling to start a project for fear of failure. Or you're unwilling to delegate. Or you linger on a project far too long because your standard of excellence is way too high.

If your interruptions come from within, vow to:

- Set goals to simply *complete* projects—not make them perfect.
- Practice saying "no" to projects that do not make a strong contribution to your goals.
- Combat procrastination with the techniques covered in chapter 2.
- Set a timer and commit to working on one project during that time.
- Block out times when you won't be interrupted for projects requiring concentration. Plan ahead for this quality time.
- Set a specific time to return phone calls or look at your email.
- Refrain from engaging in time-consuming, personal conversations during work hours.
- Play upbeat music during a boring activity, and promise yourself a reward when it is done.

Mini-Quiz

1. Are you keeping up with technology trends that can help you be more efficient?

2. Do you have any plans to buy new electronic equipment?

3. Have you created rules and strategies to control communication overload?

If you answered "yes" to all three, you have our blessing to skip this next chapter. You're way ahead of most people. At least one "no" means you can use this chapter to stimulate your thinking about how to proceed in the world of technology.

15

The Wonders of Technology

Getting Organized with Electronics

The most overlooked advantage of owning a computer
is that if they foul up, there's no law against whacking
them around a bit.

Eric Porterfield

Action Highlights

By the end of this chapter, you'll be prepared to:

- Familiarize yourself with the latest electronic products
  that may meet your needs.
- Evaluate whether you need to add to, subtract from, or
  change your electronic setup.
- Decide on strategies for handling your email input.

Once upon a time, business traveled on the sturdy backs of two strong but simpleminded burros, the telephone and the typewriter. Those burden bearers have long since been replaced by sophisticated electronic thoroughbreds that continue to change rapidly and are transforming the way we do business.

What was high-tech last year may be obsolete today. Five years is an electronic lifetime. This is the difficult fact Evelyn had to face in her long writing career.

Moving Up-to-Date in the Electronic World

Evelyn, now a grandma, started her writing career as a young woman with a legal pad and pen. Never one to drag behind progress, she had taken giant leaps forward, upgrading to modern basics including a computer, internet access, and a printer.

She thought she was driving in the fast lane, until she got together with her younger writer friends. They spoke a language she didn't understand referring to pen drives, VOIP, cloud-based servers, and more. They comfortably used equipment she'd never seen. They tapped out on-the-spot ideas on a cell phone that doubled as a word processor, then printed documents wirelessly from tiny printers they pulled from their bags.

"I guess I'll have to bring myself into the modern world," Evelyn grumbled, resentful of having another stressful learning curve foisted upon her. Still, she knew it would be to her advantage to move forward.

In Evelyn's early life, pushing the switch up turned an appliance on; pushing down turned it off. That approach made sense to her. But oh, how things had changed! The first time she pushed a button to turn on a device, then learned she had to push it again to turn it off, she mused in amazement, "We have entered a new era."

Children, she knew, didn't struggle to learn how to use new electronic equipment. In fact, they often mastered it so quickly they were soon teaching the adults around them. Their button-filled toys seemed to have rewired their brains with thinking patterns that easily accepted new technology. Learning new rules for the way things work just came more naturally to them. "If they can do it, surely I have a chance," Evelyn decided, bravely setting out to make a few salient changes that would improve her work.

Computer Upgrades

Though Evelyn had a desktop computer that still worked fine, she upgraded to a new laptop model with up-to-date software. The laptop gave her the flexibility to work anywhere. Besides, she knew she needed to gain proficiency using new programs before her old ones became obsolete.

She had already progressed from using dial-up internet service to DSL wirelessly in her home. She loved that change, which made email and internet work light-years faster. A wireless mouse for her desktop computer was smooth and comfortable, and made her feel up-to-date without having to learn anything extra.

She bought an external hard drive to make backup copies of the material on her computer. Though it was simple, she kept the instructions right beside the hard drive just to be sure she was doing it right. A hard-nosed computer geek had told her early on: "If you're not willing to back up your computer, you don't deserve to have one." Tough talk. But it stuck with her, and she respected it.

The Multitasking Printer

When Evelyn upgraded to a printer that could scan, copy, and fax, she quickly saw the benefits. Scanning and sending photos to her publisher was a convenient way to submit necessary material. She could add pictures to her social networking group page as well. It came as a real surprise to her when she realized she could scan and send documents, such as contracts. That eliminated the need for her clunky old fax machine. And getting rid of it freed up space and allowed her to save money by canceling her dedicated fax line. The new, do-it-all printer worked wirelessly, so she could print from her laptop no matter where she was using it in the house.

Fabulous Phone Service

The myriad of telephone services available now was dizzying. Evelyn narrowed down a few of her choices. Someone suggested she change what she had previously used as her fax line to a dedicated business line or simply use a cell phone to do business.

Her teenage nephew (on whom she relied for consultations in such matters) had a cell phone that could answer two numbers, one of which he had gotten off the internet for free and had forwarded to his cell phone.

She learned she could designate one ring tone on her cell phone for personal calls and another for calls to the business line. And if she wanted to check email on her phone and respond right away, she could, her nephew explained. All of this was impressive, but way too complicated for her, Evelyn decided.

She decided to stick to the basics, using her cell phone for business and her home phone for personal calls. Using her cell phone for business made sense—it would allow her to keep in touch with business needs when she traveled to speak or do consulting work. She was delighted to find that her cell phone package already included call forwarding, caller ID, call-waiting, separate ring tones, and scores of other functions she'd never used. She vowed to learn to use them, with her nephew's help, over time.

Uh . . . What's a Smartphone?

John was more comfortable with new technology than Evelyn, but he still felt overwhelmed with all the choices.

When he joined a new company, he got the standard Smartphone issued to everyone on the firm's management team. He had tried and discarded an earlier model because it was awkward to use. But this new, upgraded version truly made life easier.

Through it he had easy access to the internet, email, the company calendar that was easily updated from headquarters, text messaging, and, of course, phone and voice-mail service. Audio signals alerted him to appointments, arriving email, phone calls, and text messages. Colleagues even used their Smartphones to show PowerPoint presentations. And he knew there were websites that provided thousands of free or low-cost applications that would add to the many tricks his Smartphone could already do.

John didn't worry about losing information because his company had a service that kept his input backed up continually. He carried the phone in a belt holder, because if he lost his Smartphone (and that baby wasn't cheap) he'd have to pay for it. *Besides*, he thought, *it just wouldn't be cool to lose a source of company information*. He realized that was one significant drawback to handheld technology.

Waking Up from the Email Nightmare

Most everyone with an email account is caught in an avalanche of incoming messages. Important information that we want and need gets buried in forwarded jokes, spam, unnecessary conversations, newsletters, ads, and more.

There's also the issue of privacy. Email can be easily forwarded or blind carbon-copied, which means someone else may be receiving the same email with you—or even one you sent to someone else—while you remain blissfully unaware that they've been made privy to your information.

Often, these cybermessages that seem to hover in the sky in a mysterious vault somewhere can come back to haunt the writer. Though email seems to be a cross between phone conversation and postal mail, it's really quite different from both and requires a method of handling all its own.

Because of the nature of email and the volume with which it arrives, resolve to keep your in-box clear, and follow these tips for maintaining control of it:

- **Every time you read an email message,** either respond immediately and delete it, forward it, or transfer it to a folder for future use. Save emails that should be retained for future reference in a properly labeled folder in your mail program.
- **Move messages that require a response to an "Action" folder,** if you can't act on them immediately.
- **Store groups of similar emails**—such as "Personal," "Client Needs," and "Contracts"—in labeled folders in your email program.
- **Sweep emails that prompt indecision into a dated "Archive" folder** and out of your in-box. They're the ones puddled at the bottom of the in-box awaiting a decision. Eventually, we forget why they're there, but we're afraid to let them go.

 FACTOID: According to a study by the Interactive Data Corporation, email consumes an average of thirteen hours per week per information worker. If the average worker at a company makes $75,000 a year, the time spent on reading and answering email costs a company $20,990 per worker per year.[14]

Smart Steps in the Right Direction

Flip now to chapter 20, "Smart and Useful Ideas," beginning on page 207, to continue creating a powerful tool that can help you stay on track in your organizing by answering these questions:

15.1. Note any additions or subtractions of electronic equipment you need to make.

15.2. Clear out old email from your in-box using an archive folder.

Mini-Quiz

1. Does your office have a good feel to its organization?

2. Do you have a plan for the various procedures your business requires?

3. Have you written the procedures to make them concrete for you and perhaps others?

If you answered "no" to any of.these, you'll find steps in the next chapter that will help make your workplace ideal.

16

The Ideal Office

The quality of a person's life is in direct proportion
to their commitment to excellence, regardless of their
chosen field of endeavor.

Vince Lombardi

Action Highlights

By the end of this chapter, you'll be prepared to:

- Visualize characteristics of the ideal office—as it applies to *you*.
- Identify what changes need to be made in your office.
- Begin to create a specific transformation plan.

An ideal office, a really smart office, is one that works smoothly. Papers come in and are handled efficiently; clients and customers are handled in a smooth, appropriate way. Work gets done. People aren't stressed out.

It's the scenario we all wish we had, but somehow it eludes most companies. Fortunately for Sharon, her new company is a rare jewel that has its act together. It operates an ideal office.

Sharon, a thirty-seven-year-old computer tech with a broad smile and deep dimples, loves to come to work. She especially enjoys the environment. In her office, clutter is noticeably absent. There are no paper piles leaning off every surface. Monitors are free of sticky notes. Simply put, it's a pleasant place to be.

It's well lit and even smells good. The office hums with efficiency and has an air of productivity. Sharon and her colleagues don't have the stress of trying to find lost documents or hurrying to meet deadlines. They're able to focus on completing their work and making clients happy, instead of wasting time on endless paperwork. The work flows forward smoothly.

The clients notice it too. Confident in the company, they readily hand over critical documents without worrying they'll be misplaced. Customers sense their time is valued, and they leave with the peace of mind that their business is in good hands.

Sharon's office is not ideal by accident. There are specific procedures in place to ensure that everyone remains productive. There's a system for handling files, which dictates who is allowed to take files in and out, how they are labeled, and how the information is used. There's even an explanation of the system in the front of each file drawer. With this smart system in place, files don't get misplaced, which eliminates the stress of scurrying to recover lost documents. Ahhhhhhh.

Dealing with clients consistently is another priority. There are specific guidelines in place for engaging clients initially, working with them, and following up—they call it their EFU system (Entrance to Follow-Up). At every stage of interaction with a client—from being identified as a prospect, to following up after completion of a project—there are protocols. To know what to do for each client, an employee in

Sharon's office only needs to know in which stage the client falls. Everything flows. It's a chaos-free zone.

Workers in Sharon's office answer the telephone with a standard greeting—always within five rings. There is a procedure for handling outside calls, internal calls, email, and interoffice memos.

At first, Sharon was amazed by how smoothly her workdays went. Her previous office experience had been very different. Piles of files, misplaced documents, jerky appointment keeping, frayed relationships, and that awful feeling that some crisis was about to happen hung over the office like a thundercloud.

Sharon had to adjust to the peace and tranquility. She realized it was simply the result of implementing carefully thought-out procedures, and wondered if everyone could do this.

It all seems so easy, she thought, as she picked up a chart listing the location of supplies and equipment in the office. *When I need to know where something is, I can just look at the chart. When I need to know where something goes, I refer to the chart. It just makes sense.*

Everyone in the office seemed to know his or her job responsibilities. And if there ever was a question about roles, it was easy to check a chart that listed which jobs fell to each employee. "When I'm not sure if something is part of my job, it's easy to confirm!" Sharon marveled. Yes, this was smooth sailing!

When Sharon attended a luncheon with her former co-workers, she amazed them with story after story of workplace bliss. They were astonished, and demanded to know how her new colleagues had achieved such organizational success.

"It's simple," she revealed with a smile. "They just have procedures for 80 percent of the things that will come up; and the other 20 percent just seem to fall in place."

She was right. Planning ahead is the answer. Although we may prefer to act spontaneously, the words of ancient Chinese philosopher Confucius still ring true: "Success depends upon previous preparation, and without such preparation there is sure to be failure."

We would do well to do what Confucius suggested, and what Sharon's new officemates had done—take the time and energy to create a workstation or desk manual that clearly outlines specific tasks commonly carried out at the desk, in the office, and within the company.

Before you begin building your office manual, you may want to create an organizational chart, which outlines responsibilities and job descriptions, and list consistent steps for procedures and systems to deal with:

- **Clients,** from initial contact to the conclusion of your work for them.
- **Files, forms, and paperwork,** from their creation or entrance into your office, including how to name them, how long to keep them, and where to store them.
- **Phone calls,** including greetings, forwarding, screening, and taking messages.
- **Mail, email, and other correspondence.**
- **Storage of supplies and equipment.**

After that, it's not hard to do. Just begin by listing tasks. Then map out steps for each. Contain them in a notebook. Voila! Your office manual is taking shape. It will be a work in progress for a while. Many ideas will spring to mind as you read this book. But know this: as you create the ideal office on paper, you'll be building the ideal office in reality.

If you have a small office or you're a lone ranger, a manual with just a few pages may be enough. Even if you rarely refer to it, you'll put yourself on a more productive organizational track just for having given your procedures careful consideration.

Plan it, and your office will work for you!

FACTOID: When studying office efficiency, the Delphi Group found that 15 percent of all paper handled in business is lost.[15]

Smart Steps in the Right Direction

Flip now to chapter 20, "Smart and Useful Ideas," beginning on page 207, to continue creating a powerful tool that can help you stay on track in your organizing by answering these questions:

16.1. Which procedures or systems work most smoothly in your office?

16.2. Which tasks seem to cause the most chaos because of a lack of clearly defined procedures?

16.3. Jot down a list of systems and procedures that would, ideally, be part of a manual in your office.

Mini-Quiz

1. Do you have trouble maintaining order after you have created it?

2. Do you write notes to yourself on scraps of paper or the back of envelopes?

3. Do you have a significant powerful habit that keeps you organizationally on track?

Two "yeses," followed by a "no," are green lights for you to move on to the next chapter.

17

The Secret
to Maintaining Order

Nine Little Words

Motivation is what gets you started. Habit is what keeps
you going.

Jim Ryun

Action Highlights

By the end of this chapter, you'll be prepared to:

- Maintain your office using the proper tools.
- Create a workable maintenance system.
- Use powerful habits to maintain your newfound success.

You're getting there! If you're following the tips prescribed
in this book, your office should really be taking shape as an
organized, smoothly operating place to be.

The bad news: it won't just stay organized without any effort.

The truth is, if the art of organizing has an Achilles heel, a chronic weak spot that can lead to its demise, it's the task of maintaining. But don't despair. We'll show you how to keep your champion in the game.

It's common for hard-won and newly ordered organizing systems to crumble under everyday use. Shortly after we get the place in order, the papers start piling up again and time management goes down in flames. It's not surprising that after this disintegration pattern happens a couple of times, many office workers become too discouraged to continue putting forth the effort to organize yet again. "What's the use?" they ask. "I just can't keep it up. I guess I'm just not the organized type." Generally they revert back to a pile system, defending it by saying, "It may not look good, but I know where everything is."

That may be somewhat true. But working with a pile takes up too much time and energy. It's not a good system. It's not a system at all. Thumbing through piles to locate a paper that is, "Right here somewhere, I know it!" is stressful and time-consuming. Those piles look bad too. And if someone is standing in your office waiting for the material, you feel embarrassed and pressured as you fumble through the papers.

Never fear. You do not have to ride this discouraging roller coaster anymore. There's a clear, simple answer to the problem.

The Secret . . . Shhhhhh!

Successful office organizing from beginning to end can be summed up in nine small but organizationally powerful words: the right tools, the right systems, the right habits.

We've talked about the right tools. These include smart office layouts that allow for proper workflow and smart furniture and equipment choices that meet your needs. Once these are in place, maintaining order depends on the other two: the right systems and the right habits.

Master these and your office will work like a mint condition BMW, and you'll be the proud driver. Get them wrong, and you may end up frustrated and foolish-looking in your jalopy in a ditch.

The Right Tools: Do You Have Them?

Is your office really ready for business? Your business?

Once you have the right place for things, and you have them arranged so everything you need is easily accessible, you'll be far more likely to put things away. So let's double-check that you have the right storage areas for your things: Do you have the appropriate large tools: a comfortable desk, a filing cabinet, and adequate shelving and storage?

How about the small tools that keep you moving efficiently through your tasks? Do you have what you need? Take an inventory of supplies. Is there anything you need to do your job well? Do you need a desk tray, pencil holder, hole punch, three-ring binder, or anything else?

Office tools aren't designed primarily to be attractive. Filing cabinets, especially, are regarded with disdain. But rejecting needed equipment just because you don't like its looks will quickly result in clutter buildup, because your workflow is interrupted.

Deidra, like many women, did not want a filing cabinet—what she called "one of those ugly things"—in her home office. She was trying to get along with an attractive, three-tiered basket arrangement on a rickety stand probably designed for a kitchen or kid's room. The papers she needed to keep were too heavy for the setup, and the baskets wouldn't pull open. The equipment didn't meet her needs, so papers had started to accumulate around her office, bedroom, closets, and other surfaces throughout her home.

Whenever there are papers lying around an office, about 99 percent of the time the problem can be traced back directly to some problem with the filing cabinet. Maybe it's overstuffed, or the drawers rock, or they open only halfway, or they're off track. The handles may be missing, or it may be in a hard-to-reach location. Make sure yours is doing its job well for you.

What's been said about filing cabinets applies to other equipment as well. Go ahead and invest in an appropriate desk, taking into consideration how much room you need. Those who work with a lot of papers need a larger desk surface than those who work mostly with computer files. Is your desk the right one for your needs? Do you also need a designated computer stand?

Consider other needs. The decision to accumulate a lot of books automatically creates the need for shelves. If you have a lot of small items such as pens, pencils, staplers, tape, and glue, you've created the need for drawers, or other suitable containers, to hold these things.

Are there other tools you need? Think about what could help your workday go more smoothly. Is different equipment involved? Skimping on equipment is a recipe for disorganization and inefficiency. Consider this: if you want to put up a nail to hang a picture, the correct device would be a hammer. To try to use the heel of a shoe or a plastic plate to pound the nail into the wall would be ineffective and downright silly. So would trying to loosen a screw with a butter knife. What you need is a screwdriver.

In the long run, nothing but the right instrument makes sense. If you have been limping along with inadequate tools because you want to avoid the "ugly look" of the right tools, move out of the designer mentality into a more productive mind-set. Get the tools you need. If you've avoided buying them because of the expense, ask yourself: "Can I afford *not* to make this purchase?"

Have What It Takes?

Most office workstations would be more efficient if they had these tools:

- Stapler—and not one that's too tiny
- Staple remover
- High-quality scissors
- Pens, markers, pencils—in the styles that you like best
- Good eraser
- Paper clips
- Highlighter
- Sticky notes
- Cellophane tape
- Organizer to hold these items neatly in your top desk drawer

And when you can add them, you'll find it's helpful to have these additional items: a ruler, a letter opener, some glue sticks, and an in-box and out-box.

Don't try to function without what you need. Having the right tools, in the long run, will make your business activities more effective and simply more pleasant.

Selecting the Right Systems

A system is a set of orderly steps that support the work you want to do. Often, people falter in their accomplishments because they don't have a good system or they don't follow one consistently.

You already have numerous systems you follow. Putting your keys in a basket by the door when you walk in the house is part of a simple system. How you pay your bills each month is a system. Take the time to figure out what systems you could put in place in your office to make your work move along more smoothly. Consider whether you have a good system to maintain these areas:

- **Filing.** Is your filing system orderly? Are your papers in folders with labels? Have you created the master list that's so important? Have you left enough space to maneuver in your filing drawers or boxes?
- **Paper flow.** Have you made a To-Do Action File for all the papers that require action? Is it conveniently located for easy access? Are you flipping through the folder tabs daily to remind yourself of your priorities?
- **Time management.** Have you evaluated your use of time by using a log? Have you created a system for scheduling blocks of time for specific tasks on a time sheet or planner so that you'll complete work efficiently? Have you posted a Master To-Do List and begun using a daily To-Do list?
- **Information.** Are you keeping up with contacts, business cards, projects, and other necessary data?

Nurturing the Right Habits

Do you consistently follow sensible, time-proven habits and work the systems you've put in place? To stay organized, you have to commit to these critical habits:

- **Stow it!** Promise yourself that if you get it out, you'll put it back—ASAP. Letting time elapse before an item is returned is the chief cause of clutter. Put a "Stow As You Go" sign in a prominent place reminding you of that important motto. Following this simple rule will clear about 70 percent of office clutter.
- **Thirty-second rule.** Commit to this: if it takes thirty seconds or less, do it right away. For example, even if you can't file it immediately, as you handle each piece of paper make a decision about what you're going to do with it, and write that decision in the upper right

corner. That will save you from having to reread and rethink the issue again at a later date.

- **Give each day a head start.** Use the last ten or fifteen minutes of your day to prepare for your next workday. Clear your desk, create tomorrow's To-Do list, and remove any clutter that has accumulated. Make it a ritual, and you'll be amazed at what a difference it makes. You'll start the next day with a head start and an inviting playing field.

Attitude Is Everything

Setting up the office is, in a way, the easy part. Even though it may be hard to do, the excitement of making a breakthrough and accomplishing a goal carries us forward, making it seem less difficult.

The problem with maintenance is that it tends to be boring, because it's doing the same repetitive thing day after day.

Creative people shy away from repetitive tasks like clearing office clutter. That's why it's so important to commit to using the powerhouse habits above to keep clutter from accumulating.

You've seen offices (maybe the one next to yours) that are always in order because the owner won't let things roam outside of their designated spot, not even for a minute. Organized people don't understand those of us who don't keep consistently clear surfaces. Like dispassionate robots (and this is not intended as a slam on them), they work consistently because repeated upkeep maintains the order they love. They don't understand how others like us can hardly bring ourselves to do jobs that we don't find stimulating or interesting.

Consider this: everybody does *some* things habitually. Make an effort to work two or three of these systems and habits into your life, until they become automatic. When you see how they pay off in keeping order in your office, you'll come to value them so much you'll never go back to the old days, when you let things get out of hand.

Smart Steps in the Right Direction

Flip now to chapter 20, "Smart and Useful Ideas," beginning on page 207, to continue creating a powerful tool that can help you stay on track in your organizing by answering these questions:

17.1. Is there any small tool (stapler, scissors, hole punch, etc.) you've realized you need in your office?

17.2. Which of the habits mentioned would be most helpful to you? Make a placard stating the habit and post it where it will be in view of your work area.

Mini-Quiz

1. Do you have a satisfactory system for handling important bits and pieces of information?

2. Do you keep up with information about invitations and meetings?

3. Do you have a good system for keeping up contacts?

If you answered "yes" to all of the above, just skim this chapter, stopping where needed. If you have overlooked these and other important details of organization, take the time to consider changes you can make to upgrade your systems.

18

Tricky Little Things That Can Throw You off the Organizing Wagon

It's the little details that are vital. Little things make big things happen.

John Wooden

Action Highlights

By the end of this chapter, you'll be prepared to:

- Master the handling of phone messages.
- Make your collection of business cards really useful.
- Put meeting notes in order for reference.
- Keep track of upcoming events and pending issues.
- Manage miscellaneous information.
- Keep contacts organized for effective use.

Carolyn was moving forward swimmingly in her organized accounting office. Systems were in place and flowing well.

But then . . . her sister became seriously ill and needed to be visited in the hospital on a regular basis. To make matters worse, on the way to see her sister one day, Carolyn was rear-ended, which totaled her car and injured her back.

Using a rental car, and between medical appointments, Carolyn was able to keep going with the main part of her business, but her office (oh, her office!) quickly turned into a disaster. Papers were piled, phone calls were not returned, notes were misplaced, and work in general started to unravel.

She realized that the confusion was caused by small but important overlooked tasks in her organizing strategy. She had not made plans for some of the regular things that needed to be handled. Her emergency magnified the cracks in her systems.

This is a familiar story. It is not unusual for people to say, "I used to be organized until . . ." and then they describe an event that threw them behind. Maybe it was a weather disaster, maybe an illness, a divorce, a move, a change in job responsibility, or something else that stressed their systems beyond their limits.

There are six common stumbling blocks that trip us when our lives and activities become overstressed. Start setting up systems to handle them so they'll be there working for you now—and when you need them later.

One: Master Phone Messages

Carolyn noticed phone messages were piling up. When away from the office, she checked in to see if there were any emergencies, and noted calls she needed to return, often jotting information on hospital cafeteria napkins or scraps of paper. To solve this problem, she bought a composition book and carried it with her so she could note the calls in the order they came in. She made notes about each as she followed up.

Because the composition book was bound, her notes didn't fall out, and she could label the spine with start and end dates, showing when she'd filled it, in case she needed her notes for future reference. Voila! A system was born.

Two: Make Business Cards Truly Useful

As Carolyn squeezed business meetings between personal obligations, she came back to her office with fistfuls of business cards and meeting notes.

She decided to note the origin of each business card and any action required, along with the date, on the back.

She put them into a narrow box, with new arrivals tucked in the front of the column. Each time she referred to a card, she put it back at the front of the line. Useful cards stayed available toward the front. Those that were never used drifted naturally to the rear, available but distant.

This simple, workable system removed the pressure of entering the cards into a database or filing them in a complicated way.

Three: Put Meeting Notes in Order

Carolyn didn't have time to handle notes from meetings, but she wanted to be able to look over them again. So she labeled them and filed them in her To-Do Action File. That kept them handy but out of sight until they were needed. She put them into the section she had designated as "Not Important, Not Urgent." There they sat until she had time to consider the information, or until they'd faded in importance and were discarded.

Four: Keep Track of Upcoming Events and Pending Issues

Carolyn kept getting invitations to meetings and events, even through her time of confusion, and she wanted to continue performing her business duties as normally as possible. So she looked for ways to attend. She printed emailed meeting notices and invitations and collected them, along with hard copies that arrived in the mail, in her To-Do Action File in a folder labeled "Attend," so she could keep the details about each event handy. She recorded dates for every event on her calendar.

Carolyn put any papers about pending issues—such as bills that needed closer review and correspondence about current projects—into a hanging folder in her To-Do Action File. She attached a sticky note to the top of each folder indicating the specific actions that needed to be taken.

Five: Corral Stray Nuggets in an Information Journal

Carolyn found that even after most everything else had been put in its proper place, there were always leftovers—crazy little things that fit into no particular area of her business. She needed a way to effectively manage those too.

You have them too: stray ideas you don't want to lose or forget, such as prospective employees, interesting websites, recommended books, and so on. You can keep them in one neat and handy place if you tuck them into a three-ring binder—your personal Information Journal—or create a file just for them on your computer.

Six: Keep Contacts Organized for Effective Use

Contact information should be managed in a way that makes it easy to find—quickly! Computer software is probably the best way to retrieve and manage contact information. Some systems will automatically pull up a person's information and your files relating to them as you answer your phone to take their call. Whew! Now that's fast and organized!

Roger's successful insurance business rode on the back of his computerized contact-management system. Using it, he was able to keep in touch with prospects and clients all over the country on a regular basis. Every day, his system generated a list of people who needed follow-up calls. He duly noted each conversation for future reference. It synced with his Smartphone, so it was portable and useful wherever he was. Whether he was stuck in an airport or enjoying his yacht, he could easily conduct business. With a click of a button, he knew whom to call, when, and for what reason, putting himself in his clients' lives at the moment of decision.

Pete, an insurance agent, hadn't mastered contact management like Roger. He took a casual approach about reaching potential customers. Knowledgeable and personable, Pete attracted clients because of his affability and the length of time he'd been in the community.

Pete went into business before computer software was designed to help manage contacts efficiently. Now he was getting ready to retire, and he was not interested in learning anything new. Keeping up with prospective clients had never been one of his strong suits. Index cards, calendars, and phone message pads had been his mainstay. There's no way to know how much more lucrative his retirement finances would have been had he transitioned to up-to-date technology as it became available.

Smart Steps in the Right Direction

Flip now to chapter 20, "Smart and Useful Ideas," beginning on page 207, to continue creating a powerful tool that can help you stay on track in your organizing by answering this question:

18.1. Focus on one or two tricky little problems that tend to trip you up. What solutions will meet your individual needs?

Mini-Quiz

1. Has something happened that has interfered with your organizing?

2. Do you use a satisfactory time planner?

3. Do you give time to planning before you begin any effort?

If you didn't answer "no," "yes," and "yes," you'll greatly benefit from what comes next. Get ready to latch on to some good ideas.

19

Common Causes of Office Confusion

Even if you're on the right track, you'll get run over if you just sit there.

Will Rogers

Action Highlights

By the end of this chapter, you'll be prepared to:

- Identify spots in your office that don't quite "work right" and come up with quick, effective fixes.
- Recognize and avoid stimuli-overload.

Office clutter collects for various reasons. As we have seen in the lives of the office workers in our stories, clutter happens naturally if not specifically addressed, clogging our minds and our desire to move forward with the important business at hand.

Sometimes it only takes a minor inconvenience to throw us off track. Solve that problem, and the roadblock is gone. For instance, passing out memos, materials, and work assignments to associates by hand takes valuable time, as you track down each recipient. Imagine the time you'd save by simply setting up a cluster of stacking trays labeled with the recipients' names.

Maybe your office clutter problem is exacerbated by consistently getting someone else's mail in your mailbox. Easy solution: simply flip through your stack of mail before carrying it to your office. Leave a note for the person who delivers mail and enlarge your name on your mail receptacle. A simple solution, yet so easy to miss.

One of the winners of a messy office contest complained that his biggest problem was that it was hard to get materials into and out of the boxes he used in his office. Once he'd removed things from the boxes, he struggled to stuff it all back in again for storage. "Makes for quite a mess!" he complained.

So, how do you think he could solve his mess-producing problem? Maybe bigger boxes? Hmm. Pretty simple problem to fix easily, but it had him stymied. It's just another example of how easy it is to overlook a solution when we've gotten used to a problem.

Too Plugged In

When computers first showed their shiny little faces in the office, they offered the promise of a future without paper. This promise has not been kept in most offices.

Rather, the opposite seems to have happened. The printer, copier, and fax have made it possible for us to produce more paper than was ever possible before the computer entered the business world.

In addition, communication with others now requires more machines than ever, gizmos that must be mastered, charged, and kept from being lost. And while each one can add value to our lives and bring benefits, the preponderance of them, unless controlled carefully, can begin to drag us down and cause a disorganized lifestyle. There comes a tipping point when maintaining and using our gadgets ends up requiring more effort than they save.

Is there any way you can simplify or streamline your office equipment? Do you really need all of your electronics? Would you benefit from unplugging something? Remember the quote from Henry David Thoreau, "Simplify, simplify."

Stimuli-Overload Causes Chaos

Jane had two disruptive changes descend upon her at one time. Her company moved into a new building and Jane was promoted to oversee several smaller units of her company.

With those changes, she got a bigger office with space. Moving was a big job. It was exhausting and mind-boggling, and things didn't work as well as she had hoped.

She was disappointed with her new office: her view was now of the ugly roof of the building next door, and her assistant was relocated farther away down the hall. Adding to her woes, her new filing cabinet didn't arrive in time and she was forced to pile papers on various surfaces while waiting for it.

Try as she would, she couldn't get caught up with her work and get back in sync. She felt agitated and struggled to focus. Being the analytical type, she gave a lot of thought in search of reasons for the cause of her floundering.

She wondered if a lot of her problem was brought on by overstimulation. In a fast-paced world awash with information from cell phones, Smartphones, computers, and other electronics, creative types like Jane who love variety tend to become chronically inattentive, disorganized, and overwhelmed. She was drowning in a sea of electronic files and a river of papers, swirling with books, pamphlets, faxes, copies, and more.

Jane had bought into the fast-paced way of life. Running on adrenaline, she'd stretched herself to the limit. The office move had toppled the tenuous balance she'd been able to maintain. Without realizing it, she'd allowed her circumstances to overwhelm her organizational ability. "I don't think I have ADD," she mused, "but my lifestyle sure does. This whole society seems to have ADD."

Once Jane realized this, she quit blaming herself or her specific circumstances. She saw her situation in the much larger context of societal overload. She began to set up protection for her time and energy by modifying her schedule, repositioning her assistant's desk, delegating more effectively, assessing her priorities often, and planning more carefully. As she used her planner to balance her time use, she found that the shipwreck that had been her office began to right itself, and her career, along with her life, began to sail forward smoothly again.

Stepping into a Successful Office Environment

Good for you! You've already taken the first important step toward success by reading how others were able to bring sanity to their pretty crazy offices. You'll be able to do it too—not all at once, of course. Do it in stages. You probably have steps you'd like to take jotted down in the "Smart and Useful Ideas" chapter. We hope so. Some of those steps, like the To-Do Action File, can be implemented quickly and will give you instant improvement in the organization of your office. Do those steps first. Some, like bringing in different furniture or setting up a reference filing system, will take awhile. You may need to call in help on some of those bigger projects.

Do what it takes to follow through. Make and post a list of your priorities to keep your mind focused. Check them off as they are done and then go back to your "Smart and Useful Ideas" for what comes next. Don't let the fire of your enthusiasm die down.

While you may not enjoy the process of getting organized at first, we think you'll soon agree that being organized is fun! Walking into an office that looks good and supports you in your work is worth all the effort. You'll be productive. And happily productive, at that.

Smart Steps in the Right Direction

Flip now to chapter 20, "Smart and Useful Ideas," beginning on page 207, to continue creating a powerful tool that can help you stay on track in your organizing by answering these questions:

19.1. Which nagging little problems interrupt your workflow? What steps could you take to solve them?

19.2. Take a few moments to evaluate the fast-paced life you lead. Name two or three changes you can make to bring more sanity to your schedule.

More help is available on Sandra Felton's Messies Anonymous website (www.messies.com) and Marsha Sims's Sort-It-Out, Inc. website (www.Sortitout.net). You can also contact Sandra or Marsha for information concerning speaking engagements or personal coaching.

20

Smart and Useful Ideas

A Guide to Creating
Your Perfectly Organized Office

Spend a few minutes thinking about each of the following questions and assignments—you'll recognize them from the "Smart Steps in the Right Direction" section at the end of each chapter. Fill in your observations to create a helpful guide that will propel you through the process of smart office organizing.

1.1. Of the reasons for clutter listed above, which one rings your bell the loudest?

1.2. What can you do to minimize that characteristic's impact on your organizing efforts?

1.3. Which quick fixes will you employ now to make an immediate difference in your office?

2.1. Which behaviors interfere with your organizing goals?

2.2. What do you plan to do to overcome them?

2.3. What can you do this week to improve your organization at the office?

3.1. Flesh out that dream. Write a description of your perfect office. See, feel, and smell the sights of exposed surfaces and within storage areas such as filing cabinets and drawers. Most importantly, write out the driving force of why you care so much, and how you will feel when you reach your goal. Supercharge your dream with emotion. When that's finished and nobody's looking, do a happy dance in the midst of the order and beauty you have created.

3.2. Which of the disease symptoms above would you report on your visit to the doctor of organization? (You can report more than one.)

4.1. Name something positive about your office as it is.

4.2. Write your own personal wish list of what you want for your office in great detail, perhaps using the ideas above as inspiration for your ideas. Describe everything your office would be if money, time, effort, and permission didn't play a part.

5.1. Identify things in your office that are taking up space without serving a vital purpose. List them here.

5.2. If you were to free up space, what could you move into your office to make it function better?

5.3. Which layout would work best for your office? Why? What would you have to do to implement it?

5.4. Draw a quick schematic of your office as you want it to be. Pay special attention to the placement of the large, basic pieces of furniture.

6.1. How many small, clear storage containers do you need to quickly group like items? How will you label the boxes? And where will they be stored? Remember, things you use often need to be within easy reach, and things that are used less frequently can go in the harder-to-reach storage spots.

6.2. Make a schematic of your desk drawers. Decide which items will go in each drawer, and commit to your plan by labeling clearly. Start sorting, and enjoy the benefits.

6.3. Which items in your desk shouldn't be there? Relocate them.

6.4. How many white boxes will you need to de-junk the furniture surfaces and the floor? If you don't know, start with two multipacks. You can return the second, if you don't open it. But this job usually takes more boxes than we originally guess.

6.5. Work on clearing one surface at a time, using your quick-clean boxes. Be sure to label them in a way that makes sense for you, such as location of the original stack.

7.1. Which pieces of furniture in your office are in poor condition and are making your job more difficult?

7.2. Which items are taking up precious space on flat work surfaces and can be moved to walls?

7.3. Which tools will you need?

8.1. Because they're your springboard into action, the desk, credenza, and tops of filing cabinets require special attention. Are yours chronically in disarray? Briefly, write your plan for solving that problem.

8.2. Do you need more filing cabinets, or just better ones? Do you need more space of any kind?

8.3. Have you designated a spot to hold current projects when you're not working on them? Will you commit to putting them there whenever you leave your desk?

8.4. Can you devote twenty minutes each morning to working on the backlog of papers that need proper filing?

9.1. Which of the three types of papers cause the most problems in your office?

9.2. What changes could you make to build some organization time into your day?

9.3. Collect papers that require immediate attention in a container marked "Urgent."

10.1. If you've scooped all of your business papers into boxes, as Eileen did earlier, it's time to group them into the five categories: "To-Do," "For Others," "Pending," "Financial," and "To File."

10.2. After you finish the To-Do Action File, handle the items in "For Others," and arrange the files in the "Pending" and "Financial" boxes in a way that makes sense for you.

10.3. Set aside the "To File" box for now, until Jeri returns in the next chapter to explain exactly how it's done.

11.1. If you haven't already, create a Master File List.

11.2. Which color label will you use for each of the categories?

11.3. As you add folders to each category, add the folder name (ideally, with key words) to the appropriate column on the master list. File the folder in the appropriate color-coded section.

11.4. Stow your Master File List in the first folder of the first drawer or box of your filing area.

12.1. If you're considering hiring a professional organizer, make a list of questions you'd like to ask candidates for the job.

12.2. Compile a list of potential organizers.

12.3. Schedule a time to call your top candidates and set up interviews with them.

12.4. If you'd like to enlist the help of a friend or youth, write the names of a few you could ask about sharing the job with you. How much would you be willing to pay for help?

13.1. Do you need an on-the-go office? If so, write which strategies from this chapter would work well for you.

13.2. Which techniques could you use to create a well setup cubbyhole office?

13.3. Do you need to set up office space in your home? Where will you do that? And what supplies do you need to outfit it appropriately for the space you have and the jobs you need to do there?

14.1. Make a copy of the time log on page 161 and record how your time is spent during the week.

14.2. Block out all of the precommitted time during your work-week. Note how much time you actually have available to accomplish other things you want to do.

14.3. List steps you plan to take in order to improve your time management.

14.4. Create a Master To-Do List and a daily To-Do list.

15.1. Note any additions or subtractions of electronic equipment you need to make.

15.2. Clear out old email from your in-box using an archive folder.

16.1. Which procedures or systems work most smoothly in your office?

16.2. Which tasks seem to cause the most chaos because of a lack of clearly defined procedures?

16.3. Jot down a list of systems and procedures that would, ideally, be part of a manual in your office.

17.1. Is there any small tool (stapler, shredder, hole punch, etc.) you've realized you need in your office?

17.2. Which of the habits mentioned would be most helpful to you? Make a placard stating the habit and post it where it will be in view of your work area.

18.1. Focus on one or two tricky little problems that tend to trip you up. What solutions will meet your individual needs?

19.1. Which nagging little problems interrupt your workflow? What steps could you take to solve them?

19.2. Take a few moments to evaluate the fast-paced life you lead. Name two or three changes you can make to bring more sanity to your schedule.

21

Stump the Organizers

We asked readers for their toughest office-organizing questions. Turns out, the questions were easy. It's the answers that are hard! Some will be review for you but are worth including because they sum up steps for tackling some of the most common and puzzling problems. And if you put these solutions to work for you, they'll make you feel like you just won a million bucks. At least, we hope so . . .

Q: I'm neat, but I share an office with a slob. His desk and file are on one side of the room, and I'm on the other, but his stuff flows over to my side. It doesn't just drive me crazy—it makes me look bad too! Although I've asked him not to, he gets supplies from my desk when he runs out or can't find his. And he has no respect for my time, interrupting me whenever he feels like it. Help!
A: What you have here is primarily a personal relationship problem played out on the office organizing field. You probably have no control over what happens on his side of the

room, but you do have a certain power over what happens on your side.

Because you've talked to him without results, action now is in order. Put any of his things that end up on your side into a white cardboard box, and put it on his side of the room. As he needs those items, direct him to the box. If that doesn't get his attention, label the box with his name and put it in a storage area down the hall, making it even less convenient for him to retrieve his things.

Lock all of your supplies inside your desk under a printed and laminated sign with the words, "Please Don't Touch My Supplies!" A mousetrap might add a humorous touch. Another sign that says, "Genius At Work. Do Not Disturb!" may give him a clue that you don't want interruptions. But reinforce it with action: don't stop to talk. Most sane people will respond, perhaps with embarrassment, to these approaches and will change their ways to some degree. Your long-term solution is to change office spaces when another one becomes available. Let the new guy who moves into your space deal with the problem. By the way, this action approach works in home offices too, when other family members use your space for overflow from the house.

Q: I have a small office with a small desk. I don't have room for all of my projects, supplies, and other papers. What can I do?
A: The standard answer for a space problem: if you can't go out, go up. Get a five-drawer filing cabinet that will add filing room without taking up more floor space. Obtain tall shelves and bookcases that will give more storage room at a higher level. Keep often-used items at midrange, and seldom-used items up high or down low. A folding stepstool will help you get hard to reach items.

Q: I get a lot of supply catalogs. I may want to buy things later, but find it troublesome to keep the catalogs and to locate the items I want when I want them.

A: If you want to keep supply catalogs, you have many choices about how to keep them. Consider using one of these four smart organizational strategies:

- Tear out the page and circle the item you want to buy, then keep all catalog sheets with potential purchases together in a labeled folder.
- Put stacking trays on a bookshelf (one tray per catalog name or catalog type) and keep the catalogs you need. When a new catalog comes in, place it at the top of the tray and throw out the old catalog. That way, you'll have all current catalogs together.
- Keep a box-bottom folder in your filing system labeled "Catalogs," or create one for each catalog or catalog type. When a new catalog comes in, throw out the old one.
- Find a place for catalogs and keep them there, even if it's just a box. As long as you keep a rule for yourself— "New in; old out"—you'll be able to keep catalogs under control.

Q: I work in the public relations department of a Major League Baseball team. During the season, I'm always out of the office making contacts, attending functions, and glad-handing dignitaries. But my regular work keeps coming into my office and piling up.

A: Don't let papers pile up while you're busy. At least sort them, even if you can't handle them right away. You might want to sort in categories such as: "Requires Action," "To File," "Important," "Delegate," or other categories that meet your needs.

Then when you get a chance to handle the paper backlog, it will already be presorted in workable categories. If you can, engage someone else to handle the sorting during your busy season.

Q: I hate, hate, hate filing! I can't make myself do it. I don't get a lot of papers, but the ones I do get, I need to keep in a findable place. Right now they're piling up in my office. What can I do?

A: There's probably a good reason why you hate filing so much. Maybe it's because you don't have a filing system that works for you, and you're discouraged about frequently misplaced papers. Perhaps the cabinet is so full you have to squeeze papers in, making it an uncomfortable job. Maybe the file drawers are off center and cranky. Or maybe you're the creative type, and filing is just plain boring.

Discover your reason and fix the problem, if you can. Or see if you can get somebody else to file for you. If all else fails, use mental tricks like these to help you get the filing done:

- Set a timer for five minutes, three times a day: when you first arrive at work, right before you leave for lunch, and right before you leave for the day. File for five minutes only, then give yourself permission to stop.
- Put the papers in filing order before you open the file drawer. Then it won't seem so tedious.
- Put on music or an audiobook to entertain you while you work.
- Start using labeled stacking trays for the papers you file most frequently. That will keep them more organized and will reduce the chore.

Q: How can I get my officemate to clean off her desk? It's an eyesore for our office, and people laugh at it behind her back. She loves knickknacks that don't, shall we say, go well with my style.

A: The only thing you can do is talk gently with your officemate about it. She may not realize how distracting this is for you and the other people in the office. Maybe you could suggest limiting the knickknacks to one or two items that could be rotated whenever she wants a change of desktop scenery.

If she digs in her heels, and it's really a problem for you, you may have to get management involved. Hopefully, once she understands that her decorating style is causing a problem, she'll make an effort to be a team player. Ultimately, you can't force anyone to change their habits.

Q: How do you organize emails you need to save?
A: Organize emails into folders in your mail program. Label them with generic names like: "Clients," "Calls," "Urgent," etc. That should help you to handle the barrage of email. Sometimes specific names like "Acme Doors," "Behu Corp.," or "ColorCrafters" will make more sense for your work. Create a system that works for you, then schedule time to get these folders set up. That should help you feel more in control of your email. Keeping your email all in one big in-box is like piling your papers in one disheveled mountain. Sorting it into manageable groups is the key to claiming success.

Q: How long should I save email?
A: That depends on many factors, including legal or corporate mandates and governmental (IRS and such) requirements. Some emails are important to save, in case you need to prove something later. For these, we suggest making hard copies and keeping them in a file.

Sometimes it's entirely up to you. If you've checked, and there are no negative consequences to throwing away that type of email, by all means delete it. Like papers in file folders, most of those emails will probably never be referred to ever again.

Q: I have a backlog of straightening and filing to do. Things are literally piling up. And new papers keep coming in every day. I don't know how long it will be before I can clear up the backlog and start filing my daily mail. It seems pretty hopeless. Where do I start?

A: Always start with a plan. The problem is, it sounds like you don't have one. So your first step is to ask yourself: "If everything were perfect, how would it be?" Draw a quick schematic, placing things where they'll work best for you. Add to your sketch (which can be very crudely drawn) while asking, "If everything were perfect, where would the books go? Where would my filing cabinets live? Where do I want to reach and grab for office supplies?" Once you have made the decisions and drawn your schematic, use it like a map. Starting with any item, pick it up and place it in the correct area. Do this one item at a time until everything is in the right place.

Q: Which filing system is easiest to maintain? By subject matter? Chronologically? Alphabetically?
A: Don't think in terms of "filing," think in terms of "finding." You want to file things in a way that allows you to find them easily. For example, the best filing system for financial paperwork is by date, starting with a grouping by year and dividing that into sections such as: "Receipts," "Tax Related," and "Invoices." The best way to file papers saved for reference is by category, and then alphabetize within the categories. Think about where you'd be likely to look for something—then file it that way!

Q: What is one outstanding tip in the organizational scheme? What sums it up?
A: Here's our top four:

- Put things back in the right place when you finish using them.
- Don't store things you don't want or need. Get rid of excess.
- Put things where they're easy to reach when you want to grab them.
- Think first, then act. In other words: plan your work, then work your plan.

Q: What are the most necessary things you should have on your desk? Are personal items okay?

A: To really be efficient, you should have only the bare essentials on your desk. The fewer items, the better. Keep writing instruments and staplers in accessible drawers. Aim to have your desk completely cleaned off, and then add items you need to have close at hand. In most business environments, one or two personal items are fine. A small family photo, or pictures of your children, are usually good choices.

Q: What is the most efficient way to handle mail?

A: Here are the rules for sorting mail:

- Sort near a trash can, as soon as it comes in, even if you don't have time to handle it fully right away.
- Make a quick decision about each piece.
- If it's trash, discard it immediately. Why wait?
- If it requires action, write what needs to be done on the upper right corner of the envelope.
- If it's for reference, label it with an indication of where it should go.
- Create time daily to handle your mail, and you will never get behind.

Q: If you begin to develop good organizational skills, how do you prevent a relapse?

A: Staying organized is like developing a muscle. It's a skill that has to be exercised—repeatedly!—for it to get where you want it to be and stay there. It's a matter of doing the same things, over and over, until they become habit. Once a habit is formed, it is not so painful to do rote, repetitive tasks that need to be done in order to stay organized.

Q: I'm organized at work but can't find time to be organized in my home office. How do I find the time?

A: When we walk into a client's home office, we ask two questions to help them prioritize where we need to begin: "What bothers you the most?" and "What would make you feel the best if it were done?"

Once you determine that organizing your home office is a priority, you'll make time for it. Until you make that decision, you won't make time for it. The problem is not a time problem—it's a problem of prioritization. Once you give your home office a higher priority in your mind, you will be able to keep it organized.

Q: How do you assign categories to folders and computer files so you can find them?
A: You always want to label things what you actually call them, not what someone else calls them. Ask yourself this question: "If I were looking for this and I couldn't find it, what would I call it?" Think: "I'm looking for the _____." *This* is what you want to call it.

Often, we go wrong by trying to label things with their "correct" name. But that might not be the right name in your brain. In the case of files, be sure to write each file name on your Master File List, which breaks your files into categories. This will help you when creating new files, because you'll stop creating duplicates. And it will help you find existing files—just scan the list, and you'll know where to look.

Q: How can I organize all the sticky notes I have all over my desk at the end of the day?
A: Gather up all of the random information that you don't want to forget and put it in a three-ring binder. Label the binder "Random Information," and start keeping your notes and other random information there.

Just insert three-hole paper into the binder, and attach the sticky notes to it. Space them so that you can read each one. For random notes on the backs of envelopes and on napkins, simply staple them onto the pages you've created.

Refer to the pages in your "Random Information" binder regularly, the same way you'd glance at them now and then on your desk.

Q: When space is too small, and there's no room to organize things like you want to, what do you do?
A: Use shelves to store items. Use attractive baskets to group and gather items. If you can't spread things out, try going up. In a small office, you have to be very strict with yourself and keep decorative items to a minimum. Only bring in essentials. Use your wall space effectively with flat-backed baskets designed for this purpose.

Q: How do I get rid of the "fear" of discarding things?
A: It will probably help you tremendously to pass on items you're not using so they can continue a useful life with someone who will appreciate them. Think of giving your discards a new home. It's less painful than throwing them away, and it can help others. Give to organizations that make you feel good. For example, your old briefcase can go to a battered women's shelter or a group that helps veterans. Your old printer might help a nonprofit organization you support. A needy family in your child's school would be grateful to have your old computer.

Remember: there's more in the universe than you can keep in your personal space. No matter how big your house or office is, if you keep bringing things in and never take anything out, you'll fill it to bursting and won't be able to enjoy anything in it.

Q: What can I do with small items and papers I'm holding to process but am not ready to file away?
A: Those are good items to store in folders in your To-Do Action File system. Put items from one topic into each folder. Name the folders using verbs, such as "Resolve Billing

Dispute," or "Review for Christmas Gift Ideas." When it's time to file them, you'll be ready.

Q: What's the best way to handle all the business cards and telephone numbers that accumulate in the office?
A: The best way for most people is to input the information into a computer database and throw the cards away. Most database programs will let you sort your contacts by name, city, state, zip code, or other attributes. If you have a massive amount of cards to enter, you may want to consider purchasing a card reader, which quickly scans each card and converts it to a computerized file.

Q: I have a problem making the best decision, so I just wait. How do I force myself to make decisions?
A: The way to handle this is to look at all of the consequences of your decision. If the consequences are worth it, take the plunge. If the consequences are not worth it, don't do it. List them all out so you can see them. Here's another decision-making tool: list the "pros" of your decision on one side of a sheet of paper and the "cons" on the other. In the "pros" column, list all of the positive benefits of this action, and in the "cons" column, list all possible negative consequences. Or flip a coin. Noting your automatic emotional reaction when it turns up "heads" or "tails" will indicate what you really want to do. Then ignore how the coin lands and go with your gut.

Q: What is the best way to compact items you need to keep when you have very limited space?
A: Nothing beats baskets, stacking trays, and hanging files when it comes to compartmentalizing and storing items in a limited space. Check your local office supply store or another retailer that carries containers and baskets. You should be able to find attractive items that are suitable for the amount of space you have and your price range.

Q: How do you "make" time to clean out files? It seems to always have a low priority, so it never gets done.

A: Filing falls into the "Important but Not Urgent" category. It's a major time-waster when things aren't properly filed, yet it's hard to stop what you're doing and file when you have more interesting tasks you need to do. Commit to setting aside fifteen minutes a day to file. Make it the first fifteen minutes of your day, or the last thing you do before you leave for lunch. Only by giving filing priority status will it get done.

Notes

1. See Judith Kolberg, *Conquering Chronic Disorganization* (Decatur, GA: Squall Press, 1999), http://www.squallpress.net.

2. Tom Hartmann, *ADD Success Stories* (Nevada City, CA: Underwood Books, 1995), 17.

3. See Edward M. Hallowell, *Crazy Busy: Overstretched, Overbooked, and About to Snap!* (New York: Ballantine Books, 2006).

4. See Alan Laiken, *How to Get Control of Your Time and Life* (New York: New American Library, 1974).

5. "How much time do you spend looking for documents?" Information Management Systems, September 8, 2010, http://www.imsnetworking .com/index.php?option=com_k2&view=item&id=2:cant-find-your -document?&Itemid=18.

6. Jane M. VonBergen, "So many reasons to neaten up, but it's too imposing," *Boston Globe* (March 12, 2006).

7. "It's Mid-January: Do You Know Where Your 'Get Organized' Resolution Is?" National Association of Professional Organizers, January 9, 2009, https://www.napo.net/news/press_releases/press_releases/090109_ go_resolution.pdf.

8. VonBergen, "So many reasons to neaten up."

9. Bill Breen, "Desire: Connecting with What Customers Want," *Fast Company* (January 21, 2003): 88.

10. http://www.legermarketing.com.

11. http://www.napo.net.

12. http://www.napo.net/our_profession/statistics.aspx.

13. Judith Guertin, "What Is Stopping You from Getting Organized?" accessed March 17, 2011, http://allwaysorganizedmass.com/judys -blog/130-what-is-stopping-you-from-getting-organized.html.

14. Jon Orlin, "Email Overload Fix: 3 Sentence Emails," *TechCrunch*, September 18, 2010, www.techcrunch.com/2010/09/18/3-sentence-emails/.

15. Allyson Lewis, "Organize: Five Ways to Reduce Clutter at Work," *Morningstar Advisor*, March 15, 2010, www.advisor.morningstar.com /articles/fcarticle.asp?docId=19139.

Other Organizational Books by Sandra Felton

- *Winning the Clutter War* is the flagship of the Messies Anonymous program and shows how to start and how to continue your organizational success.
- *Organizing Your Day: Time Management Techniques That Will Work for You* with Marsha Sims shows how to take control of your life by applying techniques, principles, and tips for better time management.
- *Organizing Your Home and Family* helps you become the coach of your family organizing team. Keep your house organized, neat, and visitor-ready with less effort.
- *Organizing for Life: Declutter Your Mind to Declutter Your World* will help you understand why messiness happens to you and how to fix it.
- *Organizing Magic: 40 Days to a Well-Ordered Home and Life* presents tips and strategies to create relief-bringing organizational success to your spaces and your soul.

- *Living Organized: Proven Steps for a Clutter-Free and Beautiful Home* provides a guide to bringing out the hidden beauty in messy houses.
- *Smart Organizing: Simple Strategies for Bringing Order to Your Home* provides a streamlined, foolproof, three-point plan for keeping your house in shape.
- *When You Live with a Messie* shows how to manage your relationship with someone who is sabotaging your organizing efforts.

Books by Sandra Felton that are available directly from Messies Anonymous (MA) at www.messies.com:

- *The Organizer Lady TIPS BOOK* presents techniques and encouragement from the daily internet postings Sandra Felton sends out to thousands of readers around the world.
- *Organizing By The Book: Devotional Ideas from God's Word* lights a path for those seeking biblical organizing guidance.
- *Meditations for Messies: A Guide to Order and Serenity* contains fourteen weeks of daily reflections designed to motivate, challenge, and encourage Messies.
- *I've Got to Get Rid of This Stuff!* is a twenty-four-page self-help program designed to make a significant difference in three weeks for those who can't let go but wish they could.
- *Messy Men Clean Up Their Act* is for guys who want to get rid of the ball-and-chain of clutter.
- *Hope for the Hopeless Messie: Steps for Restoring Sanity to Your Cluttered Life* is a guide for deep-down change, and is the most personal of all the Messies Anonymous books. A necessity for use in twelve-step MA groups.

Visit Messies Anonymous at their official website, www .messies.com, where additional information about further help, including interactive support groups and a "How to Get Started" teleclass, is available. You can also learn about Marsha Sims's company, Sort-It-Out, Inc., which provides professional organizing assistance and seminars, by visiting www.sortitout.net. Contact Sandra and Marsha directly through their websites for information about speaking engagements or personal coaching.

Sandra Felton, The Organizer Lady®, is a pioneer in the field of organizing. She is the founder of Messies Anonymous, a self-help group dedicated to helping chronically disorganized people who struggle with clutter to find order, dignity, and even beauty in their lives. She is the author of a variety of books on the subject of organizing one's house and life, and applies proven principles to the subject of organizing homes and small offices using the upbeat approach that has become her hallmark. Visit Sandra at www.messies.com.

Marsha Sims is the founder of Sort-It-Out, Inc., a professional organizing firm in Miami, Florida. She diagnoses problems and prescribes solutions with a practical wisdom developed in the field, and brings seventeen years of hands-on experience to the subject of office organizing. Opening one's office door is an intimate matter. Marsha enters that door with a profound respect and high regard for those who have trusted her enough to invite her into their lives, whether in personal or business spaces. Visit Marsha at www.sortitout.net.

Have more time
to enjoy what's important!

"This book offers solid, practical advice for anyone who wants to be more productive and less stressed."
—**Barbara Hemphill**, author, *Taming the Paper Tiger at Work*

a division of Baker Publishing Group
www.RevellBooks.com

Available wherever books are sold.

Say good-bye to the stress of mess —
for good!

Get rid of compulsive clutter for life!

Revell
a division of Baker Publishing Group
www.RevellBooks.com

Available wherever books are sold.

Have a beautiful and organized home
for life!

livingorganized

proven steps
for a **clutter-free**
and beautiful home

sandra felton
the organizer lady™

Discover the best ways to bring out the
hidden beauty in messy houses!

Revell
a division of Baker Publishing Group
www.RevellBooks.com

Available wherever books are sold.

Be the First
to Hear about
Other New Books
from Revell!

Sign up for announcements about
new and upcoming titles at

www.revellbooks.com/signup

Follow us on **twitter**
RevellBooks

Join us on **facebook**
Revell

Don't miss out on our great reads!

Revell
a division of Baker Publishing Group
www.RevellBooks.com